D1384793

The Self-Regulation Model of the Offense and Relapse Process

Volume 2: Treatment

Tony Ward

Victoria University of Wellington

Pamela M. Yates

Cabot Consulting and Psychological Services

Carmen A. Long

Correctional Service of Canada

© Copyright 2006 Pacific Psychological Assessment Corporation
All rights reserved. No part of this publication may be reproduced, stored in a retrieval system, or transmitted, in any form or by any means, electronic, mechanical, photocopying, recording, or otherwise, without the written prior permission of the author.

Note for Librarians: A cataloguing record for this book is available from Library and Archives Canada at www.collectionscanada.ca/amicus/index-e.html
ISBN 1-4120-9219-1

Printed in Victoria, BC, Canada. Printed on paper with minimum 30% recycled fibre.
Trafford's print shop runs on "green energy" from solar, wind and other environmentally-friendly power sources.

PUBLISHING™
Offices in Canada, USA, Ireland and UK

Book sales for North America and international:
Trafford Publishing, 6E–2333 Government St.,
Victoria, BC V8T 4P4 CANADA
phone 250 383 6864 (toll-free 1 888 232 4444)
fax 250 383 6804; email to orders@trafford.com
Book sales in Europe:
Trafford Publishing (UK) Limited, 9 Park End Street, 2nd Floor
Oxford, UK OX1 1HH UNITED KINGDOM
phone 44 (0)1865 722 113 (local rate 0845 230 9601)
facsimile 44 (0)1865 722 868; info.uk@trafford.com
Order online at:
trafford.com/06-0973

10 9 8 7 6 5 4

Contents

4

Foreword

The aim of this manual is to provide an overview of the treatment implications of Ward and Hudson's (1998) Self-regulation Model (SRM) of the offense and relapse process in sexual offenders. This manual represents the second volume on the SRM and sets out to deal systematically with its therapeutic implications. Volume I focused primarily on the theory, research, and assessment implications of the SRM and only discussed treatment issues in a cursory manner.

Since first developing the SRM in the late 1990's, we have become aware that while it provides an extremely useful resource for assessing and treating sex offenders, it does not provide a comprehensive framework for rehabilitation. To remedy this, we have decided to embed the SRM within the Good Lives Model (GLM) of offender rehabilitation (Ward & Gannon, 2006; Ward & Stewart, 2003). In our view, the two fit together extremely well, with the GLM constituting a broad rehabilitation framework and the SRM detailing the specific aspects of therapy with this potentially difficult group of offenders.

The relationship between the two models is explicitly examined in the first few chapters of this manual so we will not address this issue in any depth here. However, we will make two general points. First, in our view a major shift needs to occur in the treatment of all offenders, sexual offenders included (see Maruna, 2001). To date, therapy has concentrated primarily on risk management. As a consequence of this emphasis, therapy has found it hard to motivate men to undertake the difficult process of turning their lives around. In our opinion, research from a wide range of disciplines is compelling in its insistence on focusing treatment on good promotions alongside risk reduction (see Ward & Stewart, 2003). Second, therapists are creative individuals who (in attempts to maximize offenders' responsivity) have tended to adopt a suite of interventions designed to motivate them, and to focus on their strengths and interests. In our experience, on hearing about the GLM a common reaction is, "But this is what I do anyway!" Despite this widespread acknowledgement of the importance of promoting approach goals (i.e., human goods) in conjunction with avoidance goals (i.e., risk reduction), the current literature on treatment of sexual offenders is almost exclusively couched in terms of risk management and avoidance goals. Thus, one of our aims in this manual is to make explicit what tends to happen in the clinic anyway!

The advantage of treating sex offenders within the GLM framework is that it reminds the therapist to keep in mind a number of critical elements of treatment that tend to be underemphasized in the traditional relapse prevention (RP) risk management approach. For one thing, the combined approach to treatment outlined in this manual ensures that clinicians deal explicitly with offender goals and values (motivation), helps them to appreciate the importance of process variables and the therapeutic alliance, and incorporates psychological, social, cultural, environmental, and biological factors in the treatment plan. This approach also bridges the gap between etiological and treatment considerations, and understands that offenders are best viewed as psychological agents seeking meaning rather than mechanisms that need to be "restructured". It is a deeply humanistic and empirically guided approach to treatment that takes seriously the fact that therapy is an art as well as a science.

Users of this manual should note that it is not designed to provide comprehensive "how-to" instructions for delivering treatment to sexual offenders. It is assumed that users have experience and specialized training in assessment and treatment. The aim of this volume is to provide therapists with an alternative model of intervention with this group. Although indicated throughout the text, specific treatment methods and techniques are not described in sufficient detail to enable implementation by individuals not trained in their use. Finally, we suggest that therapists use both manuals together in their clinical work and, therefore, they should refresh their memories by rereading Volume I before tackling this manual.

Disclaimer: The views and opinions herein do not represent those of the Correctional Service of Canada.

Authors for correspondence:

- Dr. Tony Ward, School of Psychology, Victoria University of Wellington, P.O. Box 600, Wellington, New Zealand.
  Email: Tony.Ward@vuw.ac.nz

- Dr. Pamela M. Yates, Cabot Consulting and Psychological Services, P.O. Box 38027, 1430 Prince of Wales Drive, Ottawa, Ontario, Canada, K2C 1N0
  Email: pmyates@rogers.com

- Dr. Carmen A. Long, Correctional Service of Canada, 340 Laurier Avenue West, Ottawa, Ontario, Canada, K1A 0P9 Email: LongCA@csc-scc.gc.ca

Chapter 1: Introduction

The goal of sex offender treatment is to prevent the recurrence of sexually aggressive behavior. This is achieved by altering the conditions associated with sexual offending, by assisting the individual to gain and maintain adequate control of their behavior, and by developing the offender's ability to manage risk. To provide these outcomes, the treatment of choice is based upon the cognitive-behavioral model, which demonstrates the greatest impact on reducing re-offending (Hanson et al., 2002). According to this model, sexual offending represents a learned pattern of behavior directed by attitudes, core beliefs, cognitive scripts, and entrenched behavioral tendencies (Yates, 2003; Yates & Kingston, 2005). Treatment aims to alter these factors in order to develop non-offending beliefs and scripts, and to develop and entrench new responses that are incompatible with sexual aggression (Yates, 2002, 2003). Typical components of sexual offender treatment using a cognitive-behavioral intervention include those that address intimacy and relationship deficits, problem-solving and coping strategies, perspective-taking (particularly with respect to victims; i.e., empathy), cognitive distortions, and sexual deviance (Laws, 1989; Marshall, Anderson, & Fernandez, 1999; Yates, 2003; Yates et al., 2000).

Most cognitive-behavioral treatment programs for sexual offenders are either based on or incorporate relapse prevention (RP; Laws, 2003; Laws, Hudson, & Ward, 2000). This occurs despite conceptual problems with the model, its lack of applicability to sexual offenders, and the lack of empirical evidence supporting its use with these clients (Hanson, 1996; Laws, 2003; Marshall & Anderson, 1996; Ward et al., 2004; Ward & Hudson, 2000; Yates, 2003, 2005; Yates & Kingston, 2005). It is argued that the application of RP to sexual offenders is limited as a result of several important difficulties inherent in the model. First, because relapse prevention was originally developed using the medical model to assist alcoholic patients to maintain gains following treatment of alcohol addiction, it lacks a framework specific to sexual offenders and to cognitive-behavioral intervention with this group. For example, in addition to following a medical model that is not applicable to sexual offenders, RP was developed as a result of observations that alcoholic patients failed to maintain treatment gains as evidenced by failure to abstain from alcohol abuse following completion of treatment (Marlatt, 1982; Marlatt & Gordon, 1985). Although maintenance programming following treatment is generally accepted practice with sexual offenders (Cumming & McGrath, 2000; Laws et al., 2000; Wilson, Stewart, Stirpe, Barrett, & Cripps, 2000; Yates et al., 2000), there is to date no empirical evidence suggesting sexual offenders experience difficulty "abstaining" from sexually offensive behavior following successful treatment. Furthermore, from a clinical perspective, the objective of sexual offender treatment is not to have sexual offenders abstain from sexual activity, nor to abstain from meeting the needs achieved by sexual offending (e.g., intimacy).

Second, it is argued that the RP model is insufficiently sensitive to the heterogeneity and diversity evident among sexual offenders (Hanson et al., 2002; Hanson & Morton-Bourgon, 2004; Nicholaichuk & Yates, 2002; Ward & Hudson, 2000; Yates, 2003, 2005; Yates & Kingston, 2005). The model assumes a single pathway to offending, characterized by self-regulatory problems, negative emotional states, and a core desire on the part of the individual to abstain from the problematic behavior. However, as any clinician will note, some sexual offenders demonstrate intact self-regulation and will seek out opportunities to offend, sometimes quite explicitly. Furthermore, sexual offenders are not limited to experiencing negative emotional states when they offend, but rather experience such positive states as anticipation, sexual gratification, intimacy, or a sense of personal power (Yates, 2003; Ward & Hudson, 2000).

As a result of its assumptions, treatments using the RP approach focus on the avoidance of situations that place the individual at risk, alongside the development of the skills with which to extricate themselves from these situations should they fail to avoid them. While there are obviously circumstances which individuals should avoid, such as access to potential victims (an empirically-demonstrated risk factor; Hanson & Harris, 2004), it is unrealistic to expect that individuals can predict and plan for all opportunities to offend. Rather, it is preferable in treatment to develop both specific and higher order skills that can ultimately serve to prevent offending over the longer term, and to assist the individual to seek out desired states (via non-offending behavior) rather than simply avoid all problematic life events or potentially problematic situations. For example, in treatment sexual offenders learn to identify and challenge specific cognitive distortions supporting sexual offending that they have utilized when offending. The aim of this exercise is to increase the probability that they will prevent offending in future via the development of new, non-offending thoughts they can apply in specific future situations. However, in order to successfully prevent offending and to change belief systems over the long-term, they must also learn the higher order skills of meta-cognition (Wells, 2000; Wells & Matthews, 1994; 1996) and self-monitoring (Heidt & Marx, 2003; Leahy, 2001). This is so they can better understand the manner in which they typically view and respond to the world, and to develop the ability to identify when their perception of the world is becoming problematic (Yates et al., 2000). Seeking out desired states in non-offending ways also allows the individual to work toward a goal rather than avoid a problem. Such approach goals are more readily obtainable than are avoidance goals (Mann, 1998; Mann, Webster, Schofield, & Marshall, 2004). Over time, with the learning, rehearsal, and reinforcement of non-offending cognition and behavior, while simultaneously working toward and achieving desired states, the individual can better develop a belief system and conditioned responses that will serve over the long-term.

A final problem with the RP model rests in its application to actual treatment practice. Although designed solely as a post-treatment follow-up maintenance program (Marlatt & Gordon,

1985), the model and its methods have become the core treatment intervention with sexual offenders (Laws & Ward, 2006). This represents a misapplication of the model, and has meant there has been a lack of opportunity to consider new approaches in treatment. It is argued that what is needed in sexual offender therapy is a core overarching theory, developed specifically with sexual offenders, that guides understanding and intervention with this group. In practice, this translates into cognitive-behavioral intervention that considers the individual's personal circumstances and higher order goals, considers variation in these goals and their achievement, is matched to risk and individual criminogenic needs, and makes best use of effective therapeutic techniques and methods.

Implementing Effective Treatment for Sexual Offenders

The most effective treatment for sexual offenders follows a cognitive-behavioral orientation, is skills-based, and adheres to established principles and best practices of effective intervention (Andrews & Bonta, 1998; Hanson et al., 2002; Fernandez, Marshall, Serran, Anderson, & Marshall, 2002; Marshall et al., 1999; Yates, 2002, 2003; Yates et al., 2000). It is essential that treatment of sexual offenders follow the principles of risk, need, responsivity, and clinical integrity (Andrews & Bonta, 1998; these are discussed in Chapter 2). When these principles are met, treatment is most likely to be effective in reducing the probability of recidivism (Andrews & Bonta, 1998; Nicholaichuk, 1996) and is cost-effective in that it makes the best use of typically limited treatment resources (Prentky, 1995; Prentky & Burgess, 1990).

In addition to the above, treatment of sexual offenders is most likely to be effective when it utilizes sound therapeutic methods and processes (Fernandez et al., 2002; Yates, 2003; Yates et al., 2000). Specifically, the therapeutic (working) alliance between the client and the therapist is an essential vehicle that allows change to occur via the establishment of a positive therapeutic environment that encourages disclosure and facilitates engagement with treatment (Marshall et al., 2003). An effective therapeutic alliance requires that therapists demonstrate characteristics such as empathy and respect toward the client, alongside sincerity, genuineness, confidence, and warmth (Marshall et al., 1999). An effective therapist is a pro-social model for clients, provides encouragement and reinforcement for progress, and remains non-collusive with the client's distortions and attitudes that support sexual offending. Especially important is the ability to appropriately challenge clients without confronting them aggressively, and the use of techniques to reinforce and maintain behavior change (Fernandez et al., 2002; Marshall et al., 1999; Yates, 2002, 2003). Research indicates that in a variety of therapeutic interventions with a variety of non-correctional populations (including addiction, depression, mental health, and therapy in general) therapist characteristics and approach are integral to effective treatment, account for significant variance in treatment outcome, and maximize treatment gains (Fernandez et al., 2002; Marshall et al., 1999; Marshall et al., 2003; Marshall, Mulloy, &

Serran, 1998; Yates et al., 2000). In addition, the utilization of such techniques can function to reduce attrition from therapy programs. This is essential to the treatment of sexual offenders, given that research clearly indicates that offenders who fail to complete treatment re-offend at significantly higher rates than offenders who complete treatment (Hanson & Bussière, 1998; Hanson et al., 2002).

Focus of this Manual

In Volume I of this series (Ward et al., 2004) and elsewhere (Ward & Hudson, 1998, 2000; Ward, Hudson, & Keenan, 1998; Yates, 2005; Yates et al., 2000) the self-regulation model has been proposed as an alternative to the relapse prevention approach to the treatment of sexual offenders. Volume I describes the self-regulation model (SRM) and its application to the *assessment* of sexual offenders in detail. The present volume provides specific treatment interventions based on self-regulation theory and its attendant four pathways to sexual offending. In addition, the present volume describes the application of the Good Lives Model (GLM; Ward & Gannon, 2006; Ward & Stewart, 2003) to the treatment of sexual offenders. The GLM functions as an overarching rehabilitation framework within which the more specific treatment-oriented SRM is embedded. It provides therapists with guidance on how to systematically approach and treat sexual offenders. Specifically, it provides information on the fundamental aims, etiological assumptions, and critical practice elements of effective therapy.

In brief, the GLM is a comprehensive theory of offender rehabilitation that focuses on promoting individuals' important personal goals while simultaneously reducing and managing their risk for future offending. It is a *strength-based* approach in two respects: (a) it takes seriously offenders' personal preferences and values; that is, the things that matter most to them in the world. It draws upon these primary goods to motivate individuals to live better lives; and (b) therapists seek to provide offenders with the competencies (internal conditions) and opportunities (external conditions) to implement treatment plans based on these primary goods. Primary goods are essentially activities, experiences or situations that are sought for their own sake and that benefit individuals and increase their sense of fulfillment and happiness.

We propose that the GLM provides a theoretical framework for comprehensively treating sex offenders, and incorporates the SRM by virtue of its emphasis on primary goods (approach goals) and risk factors (avoidance goals; see Chapters 2 and 3). At the same time, the GLM is able to broaden the scope of the SRM somewhat by its claim that any number of primary goods may be directly or indirectly sought through sexual offending (see Chapter 3). We further argue that the SRM, in turn, specifies the conditions under which individuals have failed to obtain primary goals and the manner in which they came to offend. This incorporates multiple pathways to offending, alongside individual variation, that have heretofore been ignored or under-emphasized in the treatment of sexual offenders. These frameworks allow for implementation of comprehensive cognitive-behavioral intervention that adheres to the principles of risk, need, responsivity, and clinical integrity, and that makes use of effective therapy techniques.

The structure of the manual is as follows. In Chapter 2, we describe the GLM and systematically discuss its basic components and implications for intervention. In Chapter 3 the relationship between the GLM and SRM is explicitly examined. In Chapters 4 through 8, the treatment implications of each of the self-regulation offense pathways are described in detail, using the case examples contained in Volume I. In the final chapter we summarize the key points of the manual.

Chapter 2: Overview of the Good Lives Model of Offender Rehabilitation and its Implications for Treatment

Introduction

The treatment of sexual offenders has developed in sophistication and effectiveness over the last twenty years or so and the field is starting to converge on the principles underlying good clinical practice (Beech, & Mann, 2002; Marshall, 2004; Marshall et al., 1999; Hanson et al., 2002; Laws et al., 2000; Yates, 2003). The premier treatment model in the area over the last twenty years has been *relapse prevention* (RP), a cognitive-behavioral approach that focuses on the identification and management of high risk situations that could lead to relapse (in this case, sexual offending; Laws, 1989; Laws et al., 2000). As indicated in Chapter 1, the original RP model has been expanded in practice and now includes the modification of problematic cognitions, affect, and behavior associated with an individual's sexual offending. The goal is to help sexual offenders understand their offense patterns, and to cope with situational and psychological factors that place them at risk to re-offend (Ward & Hudson, 2000). RP is one cognitive-behavioral intervention that remains, as indicated previously, problematic in its application to the treatment of sexual offenders. Research, however, supports the broader use of cognitive-behavioral interventions with this group (Hanson et al., 2002). The basic idea underlying cognitive-behavioral treatment is that the best way to reduce recidivism rates is to identify and eliminate or reduce the influence of an individual's array of dynamic risk factors. These factors constitute clinical needs or problems that should be explicitly targeted in treatment. Thus, treatment programs for sexual offenders are typically problem-focused and skills-based, and aim to eradicate or reduce the various psychological and situational difficulties associated with sexually abusive behavior. Dynamic risk factors empirically associated with sexual offending behavior include intimacy deficits, deviant sexual preference, cognitive distortions, attitudes supportive of sexual offending, and difficulties managing negative emotional states, among others (Hanson & Bussière, 1998; Hanson & Harris, 2004; Hanson & Morton-Bourgon, 2004).

Cognitive-behavioral intervention has long been part of the Risk-Needs Model, an extremely powerful rehabilitation theory that stipulates that the treatment of offenders should proceed according to a number of important principles. These are the risk, needs, and responsivity principles (Andrews & Bonta, 1998). The *risk principle* is concerned with the match between the level of risk posed by the individual and the actual amount of intervention received, and proposes that the intensity and type of intervention should be dependent on offenders' assessed level of risk. The higher the level of risk presented by individuals, the greater amount of intervention they should receive. Second, according to the *need principle,* programs should primarily target criminogenic needs; that is, those dynamic risk factors associated with recidivism that can be changed through intervention. By contrast, non-criminogenic needs are considered nonessential or discretionary treatment targets. Since changing these factors is not associated with a reduction in re-offending, they are avoided as treatment targets. Third, the *responsivity principle* is concerned with a program's ability to actually reach and make sense to the participants for whom it was designed. In other words, the aim is to ensure that offenders are able to absorb the content of the program, to contextualize treatment material and information in the context of their own lives, and to subsequently change their behavior.

It is clear that the Risk-Needs model, and the related cognitive-behavioral model, have resulted in effective therapy and lowered recidivism rates (Andrews & Bonta, 1998; Hanson et al., 2002; Hollin, 1999; McGuire, 2002; Nicholaichuk, 1996; Nicholaichuk, Gordon, Gu, & Wong, 2000; Nicholaichuk & Yates, 2002; Yates, 2003). In addition, the emphasis on empirically supported therapies and accountability is an impressive and important goal. However, alongside these undoubted strengths there are also some areas of weakness, particularly associated with the narrower RP model. The majority of these concerns revolve around the issue of offender responsivity and point to the difficulty of motivating offenders using this approach. These points are exemplified in the recent publication of final results from a controlled trial of RP with sexual offenders (Marques, Nelson, Alarcon, & Day, 2000; Marques, Weideranders, Day, Nelson, & van Ommeren, 2005). The RP program under consideration, the Sexual Offender Treatment and Evaluation Project (SOTEP), did not lead to reduced recidivism rates in treated offenders, causing widespread debate about the limitations of RP. The SOTEP researchers themselves have published a critical analysis of the application of RP to sexual offenders. In brief, they suggest that the RP model, although operationalized faithfully, was too highly structured, limiting individualization of treatment. As a consequence, the project did not give offenders enough motivation to change and did not allow for all relevant treatment targets to be addressed (Marques et al., 2000). In short, the program did not adhere to the essential principles of risk, need, and responsivity.

We believe this manual presents a superior model for the treatment of sexual offenders – one that incorporates the risk/needs model and its principles, essential therapeutic practices, is consistent with best practice to date (i.e., cognitive-behavioral intervention), and is incorporated within a broader perspective on rehabilitation. In the rest of this chapter, we briefly discuss the concept of rehabilitation and then describe the GLM. In Chapter 3, we outline the SRM and specify its relationship to the GLM rehabilitation approach

Rehabilitation Theory

Surprisingly, very little has been said about the nature of rehabilitation theory in the correctional and sexual offending literature. Typically, the terms "treatment", "therapy", and "rehabilitation" are used interchangeably, as if they refer to the same thing. In our opinion, using these terms interchangeably runs the risk of conflating at least two distinct types of theory and their associated referents (see Ward & Gannon, 2006). We argue that the terms "treatment" and "therapy" refer to the process of applying psychological principles and strategies to change the behavior of offenders in a clinical setting. However, the term "rehabilitation" is broader in nature and refers to the *overall* aims, values, principles, and etiological assumptions that should be used to guide the treatment of sexual offenders, and translates *how* these principles should be utilized to guide therapy. A useful metaphor for understanding the nature of a rehabilitation theory is that it functions as a topographical *map* that conveys the sweeping outline of a city, documenting all the major landmarks and their relationships. It gives therapists the "big" picture and is a useful vantage point for overseeing the therapeutic process. By comparison, a treatment model may be likened to a map of a particular part of a city that tells you in detail how to navigate within a set of streets. In short, without a topographical map, the danger is that visitors will be unaware of the landscape of the larger city. Similarly, without a rehabilitation theory, therapists will be unaware of the broad aims of treatment (i.e., reduced risk, enhanced functioning) and their relationship to the causes of offending.

In our view, a good theory of offender rehabilitation should specify the aims of therapy, provide a justification of these aims in terms of its core assumptions about etiology and the values underpinning the approach, identify clinical targets, and describe the manner in which treatment should proceed in the light of these assumptions and goals (Ward & Marshall, 2004). We propose that etiological theories of the origin of sexual offending and intervention models used in practice are conceptually linked by an overarching theory of rehabilitation (which functions to bridge the two), and argue that treatment planning and delivery should be linked to an overall model of offending. A good rehabilitation model should also specify the most suitable style of treatment (e.g., skills-based, structured, etc.), inform therapists about the appropriate attitudes to take toward offenders, address the issue of motivation and engagement with treatment, and clarify the role and importance of the therapeutic alliance. A number of these features of treatment are either ignored by standard RP approaches or are regarded as external to treatment (i.e., they are seen as a set of concerns about process rather than as comprising substance or content of treatment).

The Good Lives Model

In the GLM, an individual is hypothesized to commit criminal offenses because he lacks the opportunities and/or the capabilities to realize valued outcomes in personally fulfilling and socially acceptable ways. We suggest that the GLM can act as a bridging theory by explaining more fully (via the etiological fleshing out of some of its assumptions) what it is that offenders seek through antisocial actions.

The GLM provides a systematic and comprehensive framework for intervening therapeutically with sexual offenders of all types. There are three levels or components to the GLM: (a) a set of general principles and assumptions that specify the values underlying rehabilitation practice and the kind of overall aims for which clinicians should be striving; (b) the implications of these general assumptions for explaining and understanding sexual offending and its functions; and (c) the treatment implications of a focus on goals (goods), self-regulation strategies, and ecological variables. We will now briefly discuss each of these components in turn.

General Principles and Assumptions of the GLM. The GLM is an example of a positive psychological approach to the treatment of sexual offenders, and as such shares a number of the core assumptions of this perspective (Aspinwall & Staudinger, 2003; Ward, Mann, & Gannon, in press). First, it assumes that as human beings sexual offenders are goal directed organisms who are predisposed to seek a number of *primary goods*. Primary goods are states of affairs, states of mind, personal characteristics, activities, or experiences that are sought for their own sake and are likely to increase psychological well-being if achieved (Kekes, 1989; Ward & Stewart, 2003). The psychological, biological, and anthropological research literature indicates that there are at least ten groups of primary human goods (Aspinwall & Staudinger, 2003; Cummins, 1996; Deci & Ryan, 2000; Emmons, 1999; Linley & Joseph, 2004; Murphy, 2001; Nussbaum, 2000): life (including healthy living and functioning), knowledge, excellence in play and work (including mastery experiences), excellence in agency (i.e., autonomy and self-directedness), inner peace (i.e., freedom from emotional turmoil and stress), friendship (including intimate, romantic, and family relationships), community, spirituality (in the broad sense of finding meaning and purpose in life), happiness, and creativity. Although this list is comprehensive and illustrative, it is not meant to be exhaustive. It is also possible to subdivide the above goods into smaller clusters. For example, the goods of relatedness could be broken down further into different types of relationships. *Instrumental* or secondary goods provide concrete ways (i.e., the means) of securing these goods. Examples of instrumental goods include certain types of work or relationships. It is assumed that sexual offending reflects socially unacceptable and often personally frustrating attempts to pursue primary human goods.

Second, rehabilitation is a value-laden process that involves a variety of different types of values, including prudential values (what is in the best interests of sexual offenders), ethical values (what is in the best interests of community), and epistemic or knowledge related values (what are our best practice models and methods). For example, establishing satisfactory intimate relationships is of prudential value to offenders, treating people with respect and not harming them is an ethical value, and selecting the most effective treatment strategies for equipping offenders with intimacy skills reflects epistemic values (i.e., that capture best practice).

Third, in the GLM there is an important emphasis on the construct of personal identity and its relationship to sexual offenders' understanding of what constitutes a good life. In our view, individuals' conceptions of themselves arise directly from their basic value commitments and pursuit of human goods, which are expressed in their daily activities and lifestyle. People acquire a sense of who they are and what really matters from what they do; their actions are suffused with values. What this means for therapists is that it is not enough to simply equip individuals with skills to control or manage their risk factors. Rather, it is imperative that they are also provided with the opportunity to fashion a more adaptive personal identity, one that bestows a sense of meaning and fulfillment (Maruna, 2001), while imparting the necessary changes to achieve this in non-offending ways.

Fourth, in our view the concept of psychological well-being (i.e., obtaining a good life) should play a major role in determining the form and content of rehabilitation programs, alongside that of risk management. Thus, a treatment plan needs to incorporate the various primary goods that are important to an individual (e.g., relatedness, health, autonomy, creativity, knowledge) and aim to provide the *internal* and *external* conditions necessary to secure these goods. This necessitates obtaining a holistic and broad understanding of an offender's lifestyle leading up to his offending and using this knowledge to help him develop a more viable and explicit good lives plan.

Fifth, the GLM assumes that human beings are contextually dependent organisms and, as such, a rehabilitation plan should always take into account the match between the characteristics of the offender and the environments into which he is likely to be released. Thus, we argue that the notion of adaptive or coping skills should always be linked to the contexts in which offenders are embedded. The notion of appropriate links to the individual's life context is not new to rehabilitation practice (e.g., Andrews & Bonta, 1998). Using a concrete example, offenders' good life and self-regulation plans must be realizable and achievable given their personal, social, and community resources. Such an appropriate plan speaks to the importance of responsivity in intervention.

Finally, according to the GLM, a treatment plan should be *explicitly* constructed in the form of a good lives conceptualization. In other words, it should take into account offenders' strengths, primary goods, and relevant environments, and specify exactly what competencies and resources are required to achieve these goods. An important aspect of this process is respecting the offender's capacity to make certain decisions himself, and in this sense, accepting his status as an autonomous individual. This is in direct contrast to previously recommended practice in the treatment of sexual offenders, where therapists were cautioned not to allow offenders to participate in decision-making (e.g., Salter, 1988), and in which the therapist assumes the role of "expert" while the offender as the passive recipient of "treatment". Using the GLM, we believe that each offender's preference for certain primary goods should be noted and translated into his daily routine (e.g., the kind of work, education and further training, and types of relationships identified and selected to achieve primary goods). It is the role of the offender to inform the therapist of these preferences, which form the basis of intervention.

Etiological Assumptions of the GLM. In a recent paper we used the etiological assumptions of the Integrated Theory of Sexual Offending (ITSO; Ward & Beech, 2006) to bolster the overarching principles of the GLM (Ward & Gannon, 2006). In short, we proposed that sexual abuse occurs as a consequence of a number of interacting causal variables. These are:

biological factors (influenced by genetic inheritance and brain development), *ecological* niche factors, (i.e., social, cultural, and personal circumstances), and *neuropsychological* factors. According to the theory, sexual offending occurs through the ongoing confluence of *distal* and *proximal* factors that interact in a dynamic way. Biological factors and ecological niche (essentially contextual features) factors have a significant impact upon individuals' neuropsychological functioning and result in the establishment of three interlocking neuropsychological systems: motivation/ emotional, perception and memory, and action selection and control systems. These three systems can be viewed as underpinning human behavior and provide a scientific basis for understanding how and why people act as they do. Collectively they explain the origins of motives/goals, how strategies used to achieve these goals are selected (and why things can go wrong), and how preexisting beliefs influence both the interpretation of the individual's environments and their own behavior. We argued that biology, ecological niche factors, and the three neuropsychological systems interact to generate the clinical problems evident in offenders, i.e., emotional problems, empathy deficits, social difficulties, cognitive distortions, and deviant sexual arousal. In turn, these state factors lead to sexually abusive actions. The consequences of sexually abusive behavior function to entrench the offender's vulnerabilities through their impact on both the environment and their psychological functioning; i.e., the consequences of sexual offending will function to maintain and/or escalate further sexually deviant actions. This can occur through changing aspects of individuals immediate environments (e.g. isolating them socially) and in turn through reinforcing some types of behavioral strategies and goals (e.g., that it is best to avoid assertive behavior in intimate relationships).

From the perspective of the GLM, there are two routes to the onset of offending, *direct* and *indirect* (Purvis & Ward, 2005; Ward & Gannon, 2006). The direct pathway is implicated when sexual offending is a primary focus of the (typically implicit) cluster of goals and strategies associated with an offender's life plan. That is, the individual concerned seeks certain types of goods directly through the sexual abuse of a child or sexual assault of an adult woman or man. The GLM can explain the origins of this use of sexual offending. For example, a sexual offender may have impaired skills and therefore find it difficult to obtain primary goods in more pro-social ways because of a history of childhood neglect or abuse (a distal ecological factor). Thus, the actions constituting sexual offending are a means to the achievement of a fundamental good. It must be stressed that the person concerned may be unaware of the primary good that is being sought, and may simply be concerned with engaging in sexual or aggressive behavior in a manner that meets this need nonetheless. In other words, the goals that actually motivate human actions are sometimes invisible to the individual in question. For example, for some offenders, sex with children may simply be a consequence of a decision to seek an intimate relationship with a child, sex being a component of such a relationship. For another, the primary end or good might be establishing a sense of autonomy or power, which is obtained via sexual aggression. Thus, sexual goals may become prominent to the sexual offenders who are pursuing a number of primary goods. Pairing deviant sexual behavior with the fulfillment of primary goods helps to explain deviant sexual interest. Thus, deviant sexual interest is seen to be a consequence of learning and conditioning, although this may be rooted in biological systems for some offenders.

The indirect route to offending occurs when the pursuit of a good or set of goods creates a "ripple" effect in the person's personal circumstances that in turn increase the chances of sexual offending occurring. For example, conflict between the goods of relatedness and autonomy might cause the break-up of a valued relationship and subsequent feelings of loneliness and distress. The use of alcohol to alleviate the emotional turmoil could lead to loss of control in specific circumstances, and possibly to a sexual offense. In this type of situation, there is a chain of events initiated by conflict between goods, which ultimately results in sexual offending.

In the GLM, criminogenic needs are internal or external *obstacles* that frustrate and block the acquisition of primary human goods. The responses to these obstacles are learned and conditioned throughout the individual's life. What this means is that the individual lacks the ability to obtain important outcomes (i.e., goods) in his life and is frequently unable to think about his life in a reflective manner. We suggest that there are four major types of difficulties often evident in offenders' life plans. In our view, these types of problems are often overlapping yet conceptually distinct. It is also important to note that the real problem resides in the secondary goods rather than the primary ones. In other words, it is the activities or strategies used to obtain certain primary goods that create problems, not the primary goods themselves (i.e., primary goods are sought by all humans). An offender who has problems with the *means* he uses to secure goods may be using inappropriate strategies to achieve the necessary primary goods needed for a good life. For example, a child molester may prefer to identify and socialize with children (the strategy) in order to achieve the primary good of relatedness.

An offender's good lives plan might reveal a lack of *scope* with a number of important goods left out of his plan for living. For example, the good of work related competence might be missing, leaving the offender with chronic feelings of inadequacy and frustration. We have also found that some offenders may also have *conflict* (and a lack of coherence) among the goods being sought and, therefore, experience acute psychological stress and unhappiness (Emmons, 1999). An example of conflict in a good lives plan occurs when the individual attempts to pursue the goal of autonomy through attempting to control or dominate a partner. This has the ironic effect of making it less likely that goods related to intimacy will be acquired.

A final problem evident in an offender's lifestyle plan is when he lacks the *capabilities* (e.g., knowledge, skills) to form or implement it in the environment in which he lives, or to adjust it to changing circumstances (e.g., impulsive decision-making). For example, a submissive individual may lack the skills to assert himself sufficiently to get basic respect needs met from others.

This lack of capability may lead to increased experiences of frustration and humiliation, which may be relieved or comforted through sexual release. The problem of capability deficits has both internal and external dimensions. The internal dimension refers to factors such as skill deficits, while the external dimension points to a lack of environmental opportunities, resources, and supports. Criminogenic needs or dynamic risk factors are usefully viewed as manifestations of these four types of problems. For example, impulsivity arises when an individual lacks the *capacity* to effectively control aspects of his internal states.

Implications of the GLM for Practice. The GLM has a twin focus with respect to therapy with sexual offenders: (a) promoting goods and (b) managing/reducing risk. What this means is that a major aim is to equip the offender with the skills, values, attitudes, and resources necessary to lead a different kind of life. This life should be personally meaningful and satisfying, and not involve inflicting harm on children or adults; in other words, a life that has the basic primary goods, and ways of effectively securing them, built into it. These aims reflect the etiological assumptions of the GLM; that offenders are either directly seeking basic goods through the act of offending or else commit an offense because of the indirect effects of a pursuit of basic goods. Furthermore, according to the GLM, risk factors represent omissions or distortions in the internal and external conditions required to implement a good lives plan in a specific set of environments. Installing the internal conditions (i.e., skills, values, beliefs) and the external conditions (resources, social supports, and opportunities) is likely to reduce or eliminate each individual's set of criminogenic needs.

A critical therapeutic task involves managing the balance between the approach goal of promoting offender goods and the avoidance goal of reducing risk. Erring on the side of either goal can result in disastrous social and personal consequences for the therapist and offender. Simply seeking to the increase the well-being of an offender without regard for his level of risk may result in a happy but dangerous individual. Alternatively, attempting to manage an offender's risk without concern for goods promotion or well-being could lead to rather punitive practices and a disengaged and hostile client.

A related consideration concerns the attitude of the therapist toward the offender and the importance (from the GLM's perspective) of adapting a constructive, humanistic approach. The fact that offenders are viewed as people attempting to live meaningful worthwhile lives in the best way they can given the specific circumstances confronting them reminds therapists that they are not monsters. That is, individuals who commit sexual offenses act from a common set of goals that emerge from their underlying human nature. They warrant our respect for their capacity to change and the fact that their offending is directly or indirectly associated with the pursuit of the ingredients of a good life. The fact that they have committed harmful actions does not imply that they are necessarily intrinsically bad or destructive individuals.

Of course, some offenders are characterized by psychopathic and sadistic motivations and inclinations, although these constitute a minority. However, it is still possible to treat this subgroup of offenders with the treatment model outlined in this manual. The focus on achieving primary goods speaks directly to offenders' self-interest and what is in treatment for them. Individuals may be persuaded to change their behavior for primarily self-regarding reasons rather than because of their compassion or empathy for others. From a therapeutic perspective, it is the fact that such individuals are engaged in treatment that is critical. Thus, the fact that some offenders are intrinsically "evil" (that is, are habitually inclined to inflict severe and unjustified harm on others) does not mean they cannot be treated according to the GLM/SRM. It is simply a question of focusing interventions on promoting their self-interests in ways that are personally satisfying and socially acceptable. Therapists should be clear about the characterological limitations of this type of offender and not seek to reform their characters. It is more a question of attempting to find optional ways of meeting their needs.

The GLM, the risk-needs model, and rehabilitation theory and practice recommend that there should be some degree of tailoring of therapy to match individual offenders' particular good lives plans and their associated risk factors (i.e., problems with the internal and external conditions). What we have in mind here is that the offender's particular strengths, interests, values (weightings of goods), social and personal circumstances, abilities, and environments are taken into account when constructing a treatment plan. We envisage that GLM treatment may still be implemented in a systematic and structured way (like current standard treatment). However, therapeutic tasks within standard treatment modules should be shaped to suit the person in question based on their good lives plan, in concert with the principles of risk, need, and responsivity. For example, while an offender might receive the usual social skills module, information and material presented in treatment is personalized to that offender's own circumstances, and homework tasks are geared to his particular needs and issues (e.g., he may have a particular problem with adult women, or lack confidence in specific situations).

Another area where attention needs to be paid is to the language of treatment. Modern texts on sexual offender treatment constantly use language such as "deficit", "deviance", "distortion", "risk" and "prevention". All such words are associated with negative evaluations or negative expectancies (Mann & Shingler, 2006). The GLM is a positive model, based on the assumption that people are more likely to embrace positive change and personal development, so the kinds of language associated with such an approach should be future-oriented, optimistic, and approach-goal focused.

Applying the GLM to sex offender treatment requires the delineation of several principles that must underlie the construction of a treatment program. These are:

1. Many sexual offenders are likely to have experienced adversarial developmental experiences as children, and should therefore be seen as individuals who have lacked the opportunities and support necessary to achieve a coherent good lives plan (Marshall, 1989).

2. Consequently, sexual offenders lack many of the essential skills and capabilities necessary to achieve a fulfilling life (Smallbone & Dadds, 1998).

3. Sexual offending represents an attempt to achieve human goods that are desired but for which the individual does not possess the skills or capabilities necessary to achieve these (direct route). Thus it is possible to identify approach goals that are directly associated with sexual offending such as the search for intimacy or sexual pleasure. Alternatively, sexual offending can arise from an attempt to relieve the sense of incompetence, conflict or dissatisfaction that arises from not achieving valued human goods (indirect route; Ward & Stewart, 2003). In this situation, the presence of major stressors may disrupt an individual's functioning to such an extent that he behaves in a disinhibited manner and commits a sexual offense. For example, a relationship break up could culminate in heavy drinking, social isolation, and a sexual offense.

4. The risk of sexual offending may be reduced by assisting sexual offenders to develop the skills and capabilities necessary to achieve the full range of human goods, with particular emphasis on agency, inner peace, and relatedness (Laws, 1989).

5. Treatment is therefore seen as an activity that should *add to* a sexual offender's repertoire of personal functioning, rather than an activity that simply *removes* a problem or is devoted to *managing* problems, as if a lifetime of grossly restricting one's activity is the only way to prevent offending (Mann et al., 2004). Like contemporary medical treatment, sex offender treatment should aim to return individuals to as normal a level of functioning as possible, and should only place restrictions on activities that are highly related to the problem behavior. Thus, a man who raped an adult woman might be encouraged to avoid certain situations in his future life, but should not be expected to give up any hopes of developing an intimate relationship by being instructed to avoid all situations where single women might be present.

In other words, a more holistic and positive treatment perspective is taken than has traditionally been the case in sex offender treatment. This perspective is based on the core idea that the best way to reduce risk is by helping offenders live more fulfilling lives in non-offending ways. In addition, therapy is tailored to each offender's good lives plan while still being administered in a systematic and structured manner. Therapy adheres to principles of sound treatment practice, targeting criminogenic needs and dynamic risk factors. It is envisaged that offenders need only undertake those treatment activities that provide the ingredients of their particular plan.

In addition to this focus on a better fit between therapy and offenders' specific issues, abilities, preferences, and contexts, there is also greater attention paid to the development of a therapeutic alliance and the process of therapy (Ackerman & Hilsenroth, 2003). Furthermore, risk factors are regarded as internal and external obstacles that make it difficult for an individual to implement a good lives plan in a socially acceptable and personally fulfilling manner. Thus, a major focus is on the establishment of skills and competencies needed to achieve a better kind of life, alongside the management of risk. This *twin focus* incorporates the strengths of the cognitive-behavioral techniques and capabilities approaches to treatment. It is also much easier to motivate offenders if they are reassured that the goods they are aiming for are acceptable (the problem resides in the way they are sought). Of course, sometimes individuals mistake the means (secondary goods) for the end (primary goods). It may be necessary to spend quite a bit of time exploring the goods that underlie their offending behavior and the specific problems in their good lives plan. In the GLM approach, the goal is always to create new skills and capacities, to reinforce existing skills and competencies within the *context* of individuals' good lives plans, and to encourage fulfillment through the achievement of human goods. It is also much easier to motivate offenders to engage in treatment and to make necessary changes when they are active participants in the process and viewed as autonomous. Consequently, the GLM encourages motivation.

The Relationship between Approach Goals and Avoidance Goals

We propose that there is a direct relationship between goods promotion and risk management in the treatment of sexual offenders. In brief, we argue that a focus on the promotion of specific goods or goals in the treatment of sexual offenders is likely to automatically eliminate or modify commonly targeted dynamic risk factors (i.e., criminogenic needs). That is, assisting offenders to achieve goods via non-offending methods may function to eliminate or reduce the need for offending. By contrast, we argue that focusing *only* on the reduction of risk factors is unlikely to promote the full range of specific goods and goals necessary for longer term desistence from offending. That is, we can reduce risk, but without inculcating other methods to achieve goals, risk is likely to re-emerge. We argue that the casual conditions required to promote specific goods or goals are likely in turn to modify dynamic risk factors. The relationship is directly mediated by the nature of two types of goals, avoidance and approach goals (Austin & Vancouver, 1996). *Avoidance goals* are concerned with the modification, reduction, or elimination of experiences, states of affairs, and characteristics, while *approach goals* are concerned with the realization of these factors.

There are three strands to our argument. First, we propose that the pursuit of primary human goods is implicated in the etiology of sexual offending. By virtue of possessing the same needs and nature as the rest of us, offenders actively search for primary human goods in their environments (e.g., relationships, mastery experiences, a sense of belonging, a sense of purpose, and autonomy). In some circumstances (e.g., through lack of internal skills and external conditions), this can lead to antisocial behavior. Second, we argue that therapeutic actions that promote approach goals will also help to secure avoidance goals. The reason this occurs is because of the etiological role that goods play in offending, and also because equipping individuals with the internal and external conditions necessary to effectively implement a good lives plan (i.e., a plan that contains all the primary goods and ways of achieving them that match the offenders' abilities, preferences, and environment) will also modify their criminogenic needs. Third, it is easier to motivate offenders to change their offense related characteristics by focusing on the perceived benefits (primary goods) they accrue from their offending and by exploring more appropriate means (secondary goods) to achieve what is of value to them. By proceeding in this manner, offenders do not need to abandon those things that are important to them – only to learn to acquire them differently.

We will now illustrate the relationship between the approach and avoidance goals by way of the analysis of offenders' social competency, a criminogenic need and typical treatment target (for a comprehensive discussion of this relationship see Ward, Vess, Collie, & Gannon, in press).

Level of Interpersonal Functioning. Sexual offenders appear to be particularly prone to experiencing difficulties with social competency. These difficulties have been associated with negative mood (e.g., Marshall, 1999) and unfulfilled needs (Ward & Stewart, 2003). Most treatment programs aim to equip men with the skills necessary to foster intimacy, although there may be variation in the types of tasks employed (Beech & Fisher, 2002; Marshall, 1999). Dynamic risk factors evident in the domain of interpersonal functioning include intimacy problems (loneliness, lack of intimate relationships, and difficulty or unwillingness to create intimate relationships) and inadequacy (low self-esteem, external locus of control, passive victim stance, and suspiciousness), in conjunction with having high levels of emotional identification/congruence with children (i.e., being more emotionally open and having feelings better met with children than with adults) or hostility toward women.

From an *etiological* perspective, the overarching goods associated with social competency are those of relatedness, community connectedness, emotional regulation, and agency (autonomy). That is, individuals are hypothesized to seek to relieve feelings of loneliness, inadequacy, and fear of the world by establishing sexual relationships with children or by coercive sex with adults. While the goods sought are normal, the means used to achieve them are problematic. Turning to a child for intimacy is simply not a viable or adaptive way of dealing with loneliness and a need for closeness, as children cannot reciprocate at an adult level. Attempting to establish a sense of effectiveness through the domination of others will most probably prove to be fruitless and will only culminate in further frustration and resentment. A lack of intimacy, emotional regulation, and communication skills makes it difficult for individuals to achieve satisfactory relationships with adults and as a consequence other avenues for meeting such needs are explored (internal condition deficits). Furthermore, a history of abuse or neglect can leave a legacy of distrust and fear and can deter offenders from attempting to get close to people from their own age group (external condition deficit). This experience can also contribute to the development of sexually abusive behavior later in the individual's life. Thus, the criminogenic needs clustered into this risk category all point to distortions, omissions, or flaws in the way sexual offenders seek interpersonally related goods, and function as red flags that there are some significant internal and/or external deficits in themselves and their environments.

From the standpoint of *treatment,* social skills, intimacy, and problem-solving training focus on the internal component of therapy. The aim is to instill in offenders the competencies they require to establish the depth, range, and kind of relationships likely to enhance their well-being while simultaneously being congruent with their overall good lives plan. A somewhat neglected aspect of social competence work concerns the external conditions necessary for a person to function effectively within his social, cultural, and physical environment. This would involve ensuring that the offender has the opportunities to develop friendships and connectedness to the community via interest groups, activities, and so on. It would also mean ensuring that interest groups which promote pro-social attitudes are selected to replace deviant peer associations (e.g., gangs or pedophilic groups). The kind of social competency interventions actually delivered to individuals depends on their overall good lives plan, the type of relationships they favor, and whether these relationships are considered appropriate. Thus, equipping offenders with the internal and external conditions needed to secure social goods is also likely to reduce or modify those criminogenic needs revolving around interpersonal issues.

Human beings are social animals and are strongly *motivated* to seek the goods of intimacy, friendship, love, support, and caring (Deci & Ryan, 2000). Sexual offenders are no different but frequently strive for this group of goods in self-destructive and socially harmful ways (Marshall et al., 1999). Therefore, it is typically the case that offenders are motivated to work on improving the quality of their relationships and strive to acquire the skills and resources necessary to make this possible. By focusing explicitly on the social goods that are directly or indirectly associated with sexual offending, individuals are able to disentangle the means from the overarching goals and consequently learn how to become more socially adept. An advantage of group work is that every aspect of treatment involves interpersonal skills training and exposure to previously feared situations. The presence of supportive peers can result in a marked reduction of social anxiety alongside the formation of more trusting and flexible attitudes toward others. The existence of the therapy group is an external condition that can act as a catalyst for the development of a whole range of treatment related competencies.

Case Formulation

Case formulation (the end product of assessment) is crucially dependent on the existence of sound etiological theories. A good case formulation for a sexual offender should, therefore, outline the factors that made him vulnerable to committing a sexual offense. The etiological component of the GLM can help therapists think in a flexible and systematic way when constructing a case formulation. Its ecological orientation, focus on interacting psychological systems (including goals, and action selection and control), and attention to the role of biological variables ensures that the whole person in his environment is taken into account. A systematic assessment of an offender's social, psychological, and sexual functioning should result in good lives oriented case formulation and an associated treatment plan. The basic steps in this process are as follows.

The *first phase* concerns the detection of the clinical phenomena implicated in individuals' sexual offending. In other words, with what kind of problems do they present with and what criminogenic needs are evident? Although there are commonalities among sexual offenders with respect to criminogenic needs (e.g., cognitive distortions, social difficulties, and deviant arousal), the degree to which they are present tends to vary from case to case (Ward & Beech, 2006). In the *second phase*, the function that offending serves for the individual is established through the identification of the primary goods that are directly or indirectly linked to the sexually abusive actions. In addition, it is necessary to identify of the offender's *overarching good* or primary value. The overarching good informs therapists about what is most important in a person's life and hints at his fundamental commitments. It is strongly constitutive of personal identity, and is also a useful way of illuminating how the person sees himself and the world. It should be noted that although there is often a primary (direct or indirect) route between the pursuit of goods and offending, sometimes the picture can be more complex, with offenders exhibiting both indirect and direct routes. In this situation, offending may occur as a result of accumulating life stresses and disinhibition, although one or two of the primary human goods might be directly implicated (see the case of Mr. W in Chapter 5).

At this phase of the assessment process, clinicians will have a good sense of why the person committed an offense, his level of risk, and the flaws in his good lives plan. Also, the therapist should understand whether or not the link between his pursuit of primary goods is directly or indirectly connected to his offending. We propose that offenders following the direct route to sexual offending are likely to have offense supportive beliefs, approach goals, and marked deficits in their psychosocial functioning. They are also likely to be assessed as high risk, a factor that reflects their many years of sexual offending. By way of contrast, individuals following the indirect route are more likely to be assessed as moderate or lower risk, and to have more circumscribed psychological problems (Purvis & Ward, 2005; Ward & Gannon, 2006).

In the *third phase*, the selection of the overarching good(s) or value(s) around which the other goods are oriented should be identified and made the primary focus of a treatment plan. For example, an offender may have problem-solving strengths, might enjoy working out how cars work, and also enjoys acquiring new mechanical skills more generally. A viable treatment plan might involve him going to night school, learning how to read, and meeting with other people interested in cars and machines. Thus, the offender's social learning, hobbies, etc. might be acquired through following through on his core primary good (i.e., knowledge generation). In the *fourth phase*, the selection of secondary goods or values that specify how the primary goods will be translated into ways of living and functioning is undertaken, such as specifying what kind of personal relationships would be beneficial to the individual. In the *fifth phase,* identification of the contexts or environments in which the person is likely to be living once he completes the program is undertaken. This ecological aspect of the GLM is strongly supported by the GLM's assumptions concerning the importance of the relationship between human beings and the contexts in which they live their lives. In the *sixth phase,* the therapist constructs a good lives treatment plan for the offender based on the above considerations and information. This requires taking into account the kind of life that would be fulfilling and meaningful to the individual (i.e., primary goods, secondary goods, and their relationship to ways of living and possible environments) and the capabilities or competencies he requires to in order to have a reasonable chance of putting the plan into action. A treatment plan is then developed.

Summary

In this chapter we have briefly described the GLM of offender rehabilitation. This new theory has two primary treatment aims: (a) promoting the (adaptive) personal goals of offenders, and (b) reducing his risk of re-offending. We have argued that the two are inextricably linked and that the judicious promotion of primary goods can also result in the reduction or elimination of dynamic risk factors (criminogenic needs). In the next chapter will discus the relationship between the GLM and the SRM.

Chapter 3: The Self-Regulation Model of the Offense and Relapse Process

We believe that the GLM, with its broad focus on goals, can provide a meaningful structure for viewing the Self-regulation Model (SRM) of the offense and relapse process (Ward & Hudson, 1998; Ward et al., 1998). The SRM has been supported by at least four independent empirical evaluations (Bickley & Beech, 2002, 2003; Ward et al., 2004; Webster, 2005; Yates & Kingston, in press; Yates, Kingston, & Hall, 2003), demonstrating that sexual offenders can be reliably assigned to different offense pathways (described below; see Yates & Kingston, 2005, for a review of this research). The SRM provides a comprehensive framework for therapists in the assessment and treatment of sexual offenders within the context of the broader, overarching approach to both treatment and rehabilitation indicated by the GLM. The SRM is consistent with the principles of the risk/needs/responsivity model and effective intervention, and easily lends itself to empirically-supported cognitive-behavioral interventions.

First, we shall briefly outline the SRM of the offense process, outlining its strengths and weaknesses. Then we will describe how the GLM can broaden this model and use its descriptors as important clinical indicators of problems in sexual offenders' good lives plans. Because the SRM was outlined in detail in Volume I (Ward et al., 2004), we will only summarize its key features here.

Figure 1: A Self-Regulation Model of the Relapse Process

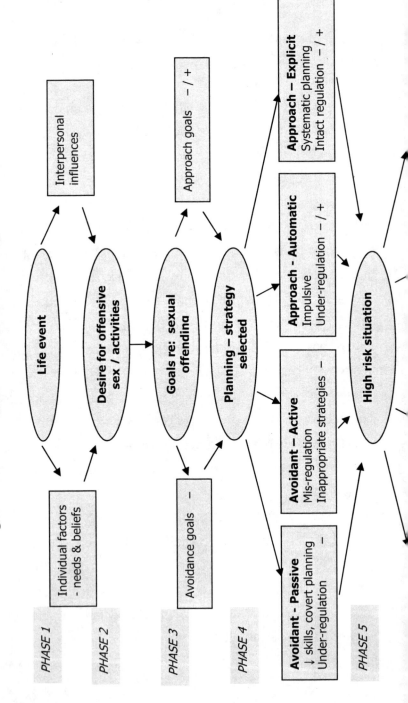

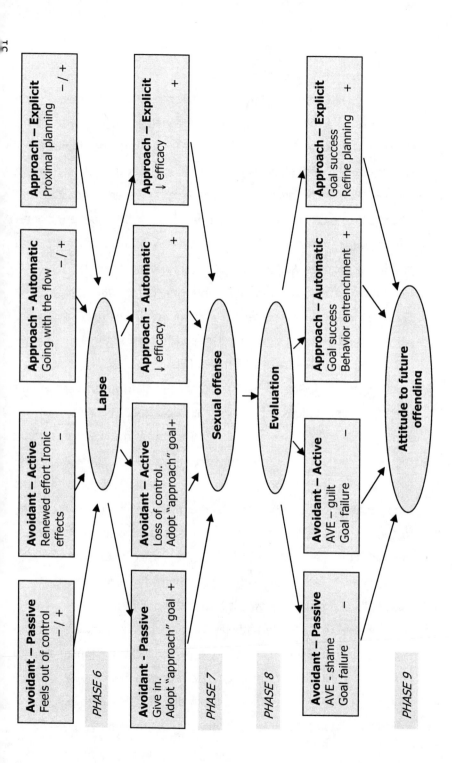

Avoidant – Passive
Feels out of control
– / +

Avoidant – Active
Renewed effort Ironic effects
–

Approach - Automatic
Going with the flow
– / +

Approach – Explicit
Proximal planning
– / +

PHASE 6

Lapse

Avoidant - Passive
Give in.
Adopt "approach" goal +

Avoidant – Active
Loss of control.
Adopt "approach" goal +

Approach - Automatic
↓ efficacy
+

Approach – Explicit
↓ efficacy
+

PHASE 7

Sexual offense

Evaluation

Avoidant – Passive
AVE - shame
Goal failure
–

Avoidant – Active
AVE – guilt
Goal failure
–

Approach – Automatic
Goal success
Behavior entrenchment +

Approach – Explicit
Goal success
Refine planning +

PHASE 8

Attitude to future offending

PHASE 9

A Self-regulation Model of the Offense Process

As previously described, the relapse prevention model has historically assumed that relapse represented a breakdown in the skills used to avoid sexual offending (Marlatt, 1982; Pithers, 1990; Pithers, Marques, Gibat, & Marlatt, 1983), with no mention of situations in which individuals consciously decide to engage in sexually abusive behavior. Later research, however, suggested that while some sexual offenses *are* associated with self-regulatory failure, others are accompanied by careful and systematic planning, and positive emotional states (Laws et al., 2000; Hudson, Ward, & McCormack, 1999; Ward, Louden, Hudson, & Marshall, 1995). The SRM was explicitly developed to account for the variety of offense pathways evident in sexual offenders and to provide therapists with a more comprehensive treatment model (Ward et al., 2004).

In brief, the SRM contains a number of pathways, representing different combinations of offense-related goals (i.e., the aim to approach or avoid the sexual offense), and the use of distinct regulation styles in relation to sexually offensive contact (under-regulation, mis-regulation, and effective regulation). Each pathway is then further divided into implicit and explicit sub-pathways according to the varying degrees of awareness associated with their decision-making strategies (i.e., passive, active, automatic, and explicit). Please refer to Volume I of the SRM manual for a full description of this model and also see Figure 1 (Ward et al., 2004).

The *avoidant-passive* pathway is characterized by the desire to avoid sexual offending. However, the person lacks the coping skills to stop himself from engaging in offense related behaviors (i.e., under-regulation). Typically, offenders allocated to this pathway find it difficult to address problems in their lives, frequently resorting to rather crude and ineffective strategies. It is evident that there are multiple areas of deficits across the various life domains – relationships, work, emotional control, and so on. The *avoidant-active* pathway is characterized by the utilization of active but inadequate coping strategies and is associated with mis-regulation. There is a conscious attempt to control deviant thoughts and fantasies but the strategies used are ineffective or counterproductive. Individuals allocated to this pathway frequently appear to have quite good general coping skills and high levels of self-efficacy. The problem usually resides in the way they tackle problems and in the use of inappropriate coping responses. The *approach-automatic* pathway is characterized by under-regulation, the desire to sexually offend, and impulsive and/or poorly planned behavior. Offenders allocated to this pathway are typically impulsive and have chaotic lifestyles. Finally, the *approach-explicit* pathway is characterized by the desire to sexually offend, the use of careful planning to execute offenses, and the presence of harmful goals concerning sexual offending. Individuals following this pathway present as rather expert in the way they plan and execute their offenses. They appear to learn from experience and have the flexibility to make ad hoc adjustments to plans as the offense unfolds. A brief summary of each of these pathways to offending is presented in Table 1.

Table 1. Summary of the four pathways proposed by the self-regulation model

Pathway	Self-regulatory style	Description
Avoidant-passive	Under-regulation	Desire to avoid sexual offending but lacking the coping skills to prevent it from happening
Avoidant-active	Mis-regulation	Direct attempt to control deviant thoughts and fantasies but use of ineffective or counterproductive strategies
Approach-automatic	Under-regulation	Overlearned sexual scripts for offending, impulsive and poorly planned behavior
Approach-explicit	Effective-regulation	Desire to sexually offend and the use of careful planning to execute offenses, harmful goals concerning sexual offending

A virtue of the SRM is the manner in which it highlights the role of agency and self-regulation in the offense process. The idea that offenders are seeking to achieve specific goals suggests that they are responding to the meaning of certain events in light of their values and knowledge; that they intervene in the world on the basis of their interpretations of personal and social events. While it is true that individuals following pathways characterized by *implicit* goals and plans are less aware of the implications of these underlying goals, they are still psychological agents capable of engaging in meaningful actions. A second strength of the SRM is its dynamic nature and the assumption that the offense process can only be adequately understood in light of the interaction between individuals and their relevant circumstances. Thus, there is a strong contextual element in the determination of offending behavior.

Perhaps the greatest weakness of the SRM resides in its predominant focus on goals relating to behavioral control (i.e., purely offense-related goals concerning deviant sexual activity) and subsequent failure to explicitly document the way human goods and their pursuit are causally related to sexually offending. From the perspective of the GLM, sexual offending is likely to reflect the influence of a multitude of goals and their related human goods. Indeed, the preliminary empirical work of Purvis (Purvis & Ward, 2005) indicates that offenders seek a variety of outcomes when they sexually abuse a child or assault an adult. Sometimes the higher level (approach) goal is to establish a sense of intimacy or interpersonal support. On other occasions, the offender may be pursuing a sense of personal power and mastery over the victim. These are all still approach goals but have quite different etiological and treatment implications.

One of the assumptions of the GLM is that offenders are psychological agents who are seeking to live meaningful, satisfactory, and worthwhile lives. The fact that they fail to do this suggests that there are problems in the ways they are seeking human goods – problems embodying the four types of good lives flaws (i.e., inappropriate means, lack of scope, incoherence or conflict, and lack of capacity). Thus, an important level of analysis when working with sexual offenders revolves around their sense of personal identity, alongside the value commitments and aspirations that comprise this important psychological factor.

A further problem with the SRM is that, although it does a good job of describing the self-regulatory styles used by sexual offenders in commission of their offenses, it gives no indication of the *causal* factors underlying these regulatory styles. In this respect, current treatment initiatives using identification of SRM pathways are not grounded in either a comprehensive etiological or rehabilitation theory.

Theoretical Grounding of the Self-regulation Model

We propose that the offense-specific goals often identified during treatment (i.e., avoidant versus approach) may be extremely useful for assessors wishing to devise an appropriate treatment plan for individual offenders using the GLM and the self-regulation model as an overarching treatment framework. For example, we have found that offenders displaying the classic pedophilic *approach* pathway to child sexual offending will be much more likely to be following the *direct* route of the GLM. In other words, for these offenders, sexually abusing a child is used as a means of directly gaining primary human goods. They may have been attaining primary goods in this way for many years. Their *approach* toward sexual offending signals the fact that they are attempting to gain primary human goods from their sexually abusive actions. Therefore, a treatment plan for these individuals should seek to promote these underlying goods in a manner that is socially acceptable, personally meaningful, and satisfying. Treatment will be necessarily intense, in order to promote a new good lives plan that overrides the habitual and antisocial manner of attaining primary human goods used previously.

For offenders displaying the classic *avoidant* pathway toward sexual offending, we have found that they will be more likely to show the *indirect* GLM route. Their *avoidance* of sexual offending signals the fact that they do not generally use sexual offending as a primary means of gaining human goods. In other words, some individuals' offending occurs *indirectly* because of problems in securing human goods in other domains of their lives. For these individuals, the desire to sexually offend may wax and wane depending on the current appropriateness of their good lives plan and their ability to implement this plan. Thus, they will need help to identify the necessary components of a good life, how to adapt a good life to changing circumstances, and how to manage appropriately when problems do appear from a frustrated good life (i.e., how to use techniques to restore *inner peace*).

The GLM is also able to account for the causal mechanisms associated with each of the regulation strategies outlined in the SRM. For example, offenders who *under-regulate* are likely to have problems in their action selection and control system. They will have an inability to control their behavior in the service of their goals (i.e., lack of capacity to achieve agency, autonomy, and self-directedness). Thus, treatment would focus upon helping the offender achieve both the internal and external conditions necessary for engaging in pro-social goal-directed actions (e.g., teaching basic internal self-control strategies). An offender using *mis-regulation* strategies is also likely to have problems in the action selection and control system. These problems will center on active attempts to regulate behavior, but an inappropriate strategy selection. Mis-regulators are thus dealing ineffectively with frustrations that may be associated with leading an unfulfilling life (e.g., there could be goods conflict or lack of scope in the good lives plan). In this case, as well as addressing the primary problems concerning the offender's good life plan, treatment would focus upon teaching him a wider range of effective strategies for achieving inner peace (emotional regulation) when frustrated. Finally, effective regulators are hypothesized to have good functioning in their action and control system – they are fully able to control their behavior in the service of higher goals. Rather, it is the higher level goals driving behavior (located in the motivation and emotion system) and the offense-related beliefs supporting these goals (located in the memory and perception system) that are problematic. Thus, therapy would focus upon shifting these strongly entrenched beliefs, so that achieved goals and primary human goods are more likely to be pro-social.

In summary, the GLM provides a way of anchoring existing descriptive SRM pathways of sexual offending within a meaningful framework for rehabilitation. The GLM explains the different good lives *routes* that offenders take to sexual offending and links these to readily identifiable approach and avoidance goals that are often noted in therapy. In addition to this, the GLM provides an etiological explanation for each of the self-regulatory styles often noted in sexual offenders, enabling practice to be fully grounded in a comprehensive etiological theory.

Our focus on the *approach-avoidant* aspect of the SRM and the *direct-indirect* route explanation outlined in the GLM serves as a timely reminder that treatment should always adopt a twin focus for successful rehabilitation. We believe that there are three major points to keep in mind concerning the relationship between risk management and goods promotion. First, dynamic risk factors are usefully seen as red flags that indicate a problem in the way primary human goods are being sought. For example, the risk factor of antisocial peers indicates problems in the goods of community relatedness and friendships. The difficulty could reside in internal factors such as a lack of the required skills and attitudes to form close pro-social friendships and community links, or in external factors such as a lack of support from others. As a consequence there may be a lack of opportunities to form more adaptive relationships. Therefore, when therapists seek to equip individuals with the competencies and conditions required to achieve these goods, they automatically reduce or modify the impact of the criminogenic needs in question. Second, the degree of risk with which an offender presents will typically indicate the severity of his social and psychological problems. For example, multiple problems and a *direct route* to sexual offending in a good lives plan are likely to suggest high risk. Therefore, it is to be expected that treatment will be more intensive and will require more time to complete. Finally, the resulting good lives plan for the offender will contain strategies for dealing with stressors and problem situations – that is, aspects of risk management or the self-regulation plan. It is important to reiterate here that the etiological component of the GLM (based on the ITSO) reminds therapists that offenders will possess varying risk profiles depending on the particular factors causing their offending. Thus, some people might have problems in securing the good of relatedness and their risk factors might revolve around emotional loneliness. Other offenders could experience considerable difficulties controlling negative emotions, such as anger, and, therefore, conflict ridden situations are likely to pose particular challenges.

In conclusion, we have attempted to map key features of the GLM onto the SRM. The GLM is a theory of rehabilitation and, as such, provides a broad framework for approaching the treatment of sexual offenders. It is able to incorporate within its structure a treatment model like the SRM while giving therapists additional guidance on how to manage responsivity and other pressing therapeutic issues. In addition, the focus of the GLM on identity construction and its relationship to lifestyles reminds clinicians that an important task is to help offenders fashion more socially acceptable but still personally meaningful identities. One of the advantages of increasing the range of approach goals sought by offenders is that it results in better case formulations and more precisely targeted interventions. It is often the case that sexual offenders following the same pathway exhibit quite different motivations while still sharing some core features. In our experience, it is often the different types of goals and their relationship to offender interests and needs that differentiates them.

The SRM works well and has gained research support, since it adequately captures the offense pathways and risk that offenders exhibit (see Ward et al., 2004; Yates & Kingston, 2005). The focus on approach goals and the strategies used to achieve these resonates with the basic assumption of the GLM that human beings are creatures who have evolved to actively pursue a suite of valued activities and experiences (primary goods). In order to effectively secure these goods, it is necessary to possess a range of internal and external conditions (essentially capabilities and resources). The two avoidance goal pathways of the SRM are likely to reflect an indirect relationship between the pursuit of these goods and sexual offending, while the two approach goal pathways are likely to indicate a direct route to offending. Once therapists have allocated individuals to the pathways using the assessment strategies outlined in Volume I, they can use the resources of the GLM and the material in this manual to fine-tune their case formulation and subsequent treatment efforts.

Summary

In this chapter we have outlined the relationship between the GLM and the SRM, and demonstrated that the two fit together nicely. In the next chapter, we apply the SRM to the treatment of sexual offenders and outline the general approach for each of the four pathways. In chapters five through eight we examine each pathway in considerable depth, systematically unpacking the therapeutic implications of using the SRM with each category of offenders, using the case examples described in Volume I.

Chapter 4: Treatment Implications of the
Self-Regulation Model: An Overview

The rehabilitation of offenders is an evaluative and capability-building process that is concerned with promoting primary goods and managing risk. At the heart of this process are the construction of more adaptive identities and the acquisition of capabilities that enable offenders to secure important valued goods in their post release-environments. Treatment within the SRM is consistent with the features of effective intervention. The nesting of the SRM within the GLM rehabilitation theory provides therapists with additional resources upon which to draw when planning and delivering treatment. In particular, the twin focus on goods promotion and risk management makes it easier to motivate individuals to engage in the difficult process of change. A self-regulation approach not only focuses on problem areas, but also on the individual's strengths, pre-existing abilities, and overall life context and objectives. For example, in addition to targeting skills deficits, this approach to treatment explicitly includes the development of approach goals to pro-social behavior, which are more readily attained than avoidance goals (Mann, 1998). That is, in attempting to prevent a return to sexual offending behavior, it is easier for offenders to approach and successfully achieve pro-social goals than it is to sustain avoidance of problematic situations over the long-term. Within this orientation, pro-social non-offending skills that are encouraged and reinforced are more likely to become entrenched in the individual's behavioral repertoire than are avoidance behaviors (Yates, 2003).

Research conducted to date on the self-regulation model supports the existence of different pathways to offending, and provides preliminary evidence that pathways are differentially associated with risk and with known dynamic risk factors for sexual offending (Ward et al., 2004; Yates, 2003; Yates & Kingston, 2005; Yates & Kingston, in press). As indicated above, the risk and need principles of effective intervention indicate that treatment is most effective when it is varied in accordance with assessed risk, when it targets appropriate criminogenic needs, and when it attends to responsivity factors. Using the GLM framework, treatment also identifies the individual's life goals, incorporating treatment change within the context of these life objectives and higher-order goals. Reducing the influence of dynamic risk factors can occur as a consequence of promoting approach goals such as the establishment of intimate relationships, as well as via direct targeting in treatment. As such, treatment should not only vary in accordance with risk and need, but also with pathways to offending. The remainder of this chapter deals with the application of these principles to differential treatment based on pathways to offending. Chapters 5 through 8 provide examples of intervention with the case examples described in Volume I of this series.

Treatment Framework

From the perspective of the GLM-SRM, treatment for sexual offenders is essentially about equipping them to live rewarding lives that do not result in harm to others. Offenders are viewed as psychological agents who have directly or indirectly sought certain goods through the means of sexually abusive behavior. The goal of treatment is to help them to articulate their significant goals and, taking into account preferences, priorities, abilities, and ecological variables, to develop a treatment plan that is likely to result in the formation of a new personal identify and more satisfying life. The goal of treatment is to help offenders acquire the *internal* and *external* conditions they require in order to put this plan into action; it is essentially about designing a new life. The major stress should be on the selection of suitable secondary or instrumental goods to be utilized by a person to realize certain primary goods, such as type of work, training, relationships, hobbies, and so on.

The end product of treatment, in addition to reducing risk and eliminating or reducing the influence of dynamic risk factors, is the development of a self-regulation/offense prevention plan. This plan should focus on two related but distinct goals: (a) the implementation of a map for living within a specific community and circumstances that possesses all the ingredients of a good lives plan, and (b) the identification of strategies for responding to problematic situations in which the smooth functioning of the offender's life is disrupted or threatened in some manner. In terms of the latter, the presence of acute risk factors that are salient for a given individual, such as relationship conflict, emotional distress, or a significant life event, in addition to signaling a potential change in risk, should be viewed as markers indicating problems in the conditions required to live a good life. While these conditions may typically be external, they may sometimes signal difficulties in some aspects of a person's psychological functioning. The skills, beliefs, attitudes, and resources acquired during therapy can then be used to: (a) reflect on the nature of the disruption threat, (b) construct an action plan to resolve the threat or problems, and (c) implement the plan and evaluate its effectiveness. When this occurs, the offender needs to ensure he keeps in mind the importance of maintaining approach goals and risk management strategies in any modification to his good lives plan. The danger of making *ad hoc* adjustments to the plan is that these adjustments may restrict access to important goods. An unforeseen consequence of such adjustments may be to reopen a route to re-offending. Thus, when making adjustments, therapists need to ensure they evaluate, in collaboration with the offender, the implications for the good lives plan, and also adjust this accordingly in order to ensure that goods may still be achieved.

Treatment begins with the comprehensive assessment of static and dynamic risk, the individual's good lives goals, and his self-regulation pathway to offending. This assessment is used to determine treatment intensity requirements and to develop an individualized treatment plan to target dynamic risk factors for each offender. In tailoring treatment further to incorporate self-regulation pathways, treatment plans are based upon both offenders' goals with respect to offending (i.e., avoidance versus approach goals) and the strategies utilized in the offense progression, based on assessment of these as indicated in Volume I. Goals represent desired states or situations that are based on existing values, beliefs, and cognitive schema. Goals are developed throughout the individual's life and are based on various experiences. Goals function to direct planning, implementation, and evaluation of behavior. Goals further influence attention to external stimuli and the interpretation of these stimuli, and are either avoidance-based (inhibitory) or approached-based (acquisitional). Strategies represent the means or methods selected by individuals to achieve goals in a given situation, and may be passive, active, automatic, or explicit in nature, depending upon the self-regulation style exhibited by the individual. Primary human goods, which constitute the most abstract type of goals that are evident in individuals' lifestyles and offending, are also evaluated at this stage of treatment. Thus, at the outset of treatment, therapists ascertain offenders' basic set of values and primary goods that are important for achieving high levels of well-being for the offender. Instrumental goods (i.e., the means of securing primary human goods) are also evaluated. It is typically here that problems arise and manifest as criminogenic needs.

In addition to the features described above, offenders' strengths are assessed in order that these pre-existing skills may be reinforced and entrenched during treatment and supervision. Also, offenders' good life goals are assessed, in order that treatment and change-oriented goals may be incorporated into offenders' overarching life and personal goals, and to ensure integration of treatment change into this schema.

Recommended treatment and intervention strategies for each of the four self-regulation pathways (avoidant-passive, avoidant-active, approach-automatic, and approach-explicit) is provided below. These recommendations should be reviewed in conjunction with the descriptions of each pathway and the nine phases of the offense progression as described in Volume I and as shown in Figure 1.

Treatment of Offenders following the Avoidant-passive Pathway

The avoidant-passive pathway represents an under-regulation pathway, in which the individual desires to avoid sexual offending (an inhibitory goal) but lacks the requisite skills to prevent offending. The individual tends not to actively engage in activities that would prevent offending, or simply attempts to deny urges or to distract himself in order to avoid engaging in the undesired behavior. From a GLM perspective, the route to offending is likely to be indirect and is likely to occur as a consequence of goal conflict and coping skill deficits.

When individuals following an avoidant-passive pathway are confronted with a life situation that triggers the desire to offend or that places them at risk to offend, they experience a loss of control or disinhibition, resulting from negative affective states and a lack of adequate strategies to control the desire for deviant or offensive sexual activity. These offenders typically have low self-efficacy expectations regarding their ability to refrain from offending, experience negative affective states associated with offending behavior and with the desire to offend, and covertly, rather than overtly, plan their offenses. This covert planning may entail decision-making that exposes the individual to situations that place him at risk and which facilitates cognitive distortions that serve to justify offending, allowing the offender to continue in the offense progression. Although negative emotional states are associated with offending behavior, these individuals may also simultaneously experience positive emotional states related to anticipation of offending, such as sexual gratification or meeting intimacy needs (i.e., achieving goods).

Following the commission of the offense, these individuals typically experience additional negative emotional states, such as shame or a sense of failure with respect to achieving goals. They are likely to evaluate the sexual offense as a negative event and to make commitments to reinforce their avoidance goal in the future. However, because they lack the skills required to refrain from offending, they are at risk to commit another sexual offense. This process of post-offense evaluation and reiteration of commitment to goals can result in further cognitive distortions that justify the offense as exceptional or as an aberration. It is also noted that the experience of sexual offending over time can result in a change to an approach pathway during future offenses, via reinforcement of behavior.

With respect to etiological factors, it is likely that individuals will lack the internal (i.e., skills, attitudes, beliefs) and external conditions (i.e., supports, opportunities, and resources) to achieve important goods in personally meaningful and pro-social ways. For example, they may lack the emotional competency skills to identify and effectively regulate negative emotional states, or may seek intimacy through destructive relationships of various kinds. In addition, their personal identity may be associated with dysfunctional activities and circumstances. For example, offenders may view themselves as hapless victims of others or as refugees from a terrifying and punishing world.

The first step in treatment with offenders following an avoidant-passive pathway is to examine both higher order good lives goals alongside the longstanding factors that make them vulnerable to offending (Phase I), of which they are unlikely to be aware. This lack of awareness results in an inability to cope with situations that trigger desires associated with offending. This lack of awareness may also be associated with the individual being in the precontemplative stage of change, although not necessarily, as some individuals following this pathway may be aware that there is a problem with which they are unable to cope (i.e., they may be in the contemplative stage of change; DiClemente, 1991; Prochaska & DiClemente, 1982; 1986). Thus, assessment of stage of change prior to commencing treatment will assist in directing specific intervention strategies.

Some examples of longstanding (chronic) vulnerability factors include difficulty establishing adequate intimate and social relationships, chronic negative affect (such as low self-esteem or feelings of worthlessness), social discomfort, inability to regulate mood, inability to identify and solve problems, deviant sexual interest or preference, and the inability to meet overarching life goals and core needs. These features point to problems in the ways the primary human goods of relatedness, emotional control, autonomy, pleasure, and mastery are achieved. A case formulation (essentially a clinical explanation concerning an offender's existing problems and their causes) should be developed using the additional resources of the GLM and the SRM, in the context of the individual's own personal circumstances.

Assisting the individual to identify both goals and vulnerability factors may be done through an exercise such as a disclosure, during which the offender describes pertinent life experiences that have resulted in these chronic difficulties, and of those situations that have, in the past, triggered the desire for offending behavior. This analysis includes identification of life goals (although analysis of the relationship and links between these good lives goals and offending behavior is done later in treatment). It is essential that this analysis also takes into account the individual's social and cultural context. It is important that the offender understand that the aim of such an exercise is not a simple recitation of factual information, but rather that its purpose is to develop an understanding of key experiences and events and their impact on the individual's present level of functioning. In assessing the success of such an exercise, the treatment provider attends to the identification of relevant factors as evaluated during pre-treatment assessment. That is, the therapist should ensure that the offender has assessed and analyzed those factors identified during the assessment phase. If the individual has failed to identify some of these factors, the therapist should reinforce his efforts and use strategies such as open-ended and Socratic questioning techniques (Beck, 1995; Beck, Rush, Shaw, & Emery, 1979; Newman, 2003) to enable him to elaborate and discover additional pertinent factors, and to link these to his current functioning.

The next step in treatment with avoidant-passive offenders involves identification of situations that initiate the offense progression, the manner in which he perceives and interprets these events based on his core level beliefs, and the specific nature of the desire for offense-related behaviors (Phase 2). The aim of treatment at this phase is to: (a) increase the offender's awareness of the manner in which he interprets events based on core beliefs; (b) determine precisely what it is that he desires to achieve; that is, his personal goals (often a mixture of general avoidance and approach goals related to his basic value commitments, etc.), and (c) link offense-related experiences to chronic vulnerability factors.

To illustrate, an offender for whom an event activated core beliefs that he is unworthy of relationships, and triggered a desire for intimacy and the alleviation of loneliness, would be assisted to identify these core beliefs, the manner in which these were triggered by offense-related events, and the resultant goals. Treatment then validates the desire (if appropriate, e.g., intimacy) and identifies both the individual's strengths in this area as well as deficits in the strategies used to achieve the desired end. Deficits can include such factors as the inability to cope with negative emotional states (e.g., loneliness), inability to tolerate and counteract low-self esteem or self-worth, or the inability to control deviant sexual interests. Strengths can include factors such as the pre-existing ability to form age-appropriate relationships (intimate and/or social), and the ability (on some occasions) to control deviant sexual desire. The assessment of strengths should also include identifying the instrumental goods (means) by which offenders seek primary goods such as intimacy or mastery and control. Additionally, it is important to discover what an individual values most – what are his overarching goods? This is likely to be directly linked to his basic sense of self-worth and identity.

Dynamic risk factors function as red flags indicating problems in important domains of an individual's functioning and can help therapists to target problems in the way he has been seeking important personal goals (i.e., primary goods). For example, the risk factor of impulsivity points to problems in achieving the good of autonomy, while the risk factor of intimacy deficits suggests difficulties in effectively establishing functional personal relationships. It is necessary to go beyond the fact that individuals have problems in certain domains and to specifically isolate whether the underlying causes reside in internal or external factors (probably both).

Treatment reinforces and builds upon these existing skills. Furthermore, it serve to help offenders acquire the capabilities they require to achieve things that are personally meaningful and important, while at the same time reducing their risk for further offending (see Ward, Mann, & Gannon, in press). Treatment of skills deficits is done through rehearsal of both cognitive and behavioral responses to events that trigger negative affect. The individual would rehearse (by stating out loud) challenges to core beliefs, and the development and rehearsal of strategies to deal with negative affect, and rehearse (via role-play and/or in actual situations) effectively establishing relationships and dealing appropriately with the desire. If applicable, techniques to control deviant sexual arousal and to increase appropriate arousal (i.e., arousal reconditioning) would also be included. The individual should be provided with the opportunity to have success experiences that reinforce skills, so as to develop and entrench these skills.

For the avoidant-passive offender, the individual's goals with respect to avoiding offending should be reinforced and validated (Phase 3). For this individual, the primary focus of treatment rests with the strategies selected to achieve this goal (Phase 4), which are lacking. In addition, a plan for living a better, more satisfying life is used to structure the implementation of such deficit modifying treatment approaches. It is not enough to equip an offender allocated to the avoidant-passive pathway to resist and control his deviant urges. It is imperative to ask exactly what is he seeking via sex with children or the sexual assault of adults. Is it intimacy, emotional relief, pleasure, novelty, play, domination/autonomy, mastery, and so on? The therapist then uses this information to ensure that important goals are factored into a plan, and that the individual acquires the internal (i.e., capabilities) and external (i.e., support, opportunities, resources) means to achieve these important outcomes. Of course, any plan always takes into account the external (release environment, degree of support, work opportunities, etc.) and internal (abilities, temperament, physical/medical problems, etc.) constraints confronting each offender. It is important to be pragmatic without being overly reductionistic in our aspirations for offenders' lives.

Treatment at this phase assists the offender to develop an understanding of the manner in which control is lost when confronted with a situation that triggers the desire to offend. For example, an offender who simply ignores his sexual urges would be assisted in coming to the realization that, while this may have been temporarily effective, the desires and needs remain. Treatment then aims to assist the individual to generate strategies that would be effective in maintaining control, and to subsequently rehearse and entrench these strategies. Simultaneously, treatment would assist in the development and reinforcement of strategies to meet appropriate needs in an acceptable manner – that is, to achieve the range of goods specified for the individual. Since these individuals desire to avoid offending, developing an understanding of the victim's experience (perspective-taking/empathy) and entrenching this understanding is also part of the treatment strategy with these offenders. It is noted, however, that offenders following this pathway are likely have at least a rudimentary understanding of the victim's experience, given that they desire to avoid offending.

For this pathway, treatment at Phase 5 would assist the individual in understanding that, when faced with a high risk situation, he experiences a loss of control, that in turn results in him abandoning his avoidance goal, adopting an approach goal, and, subsequently, offending (Phases 6 and 7). Treatment focuses on identifying the specific processes by which the individual abandoned the avoidance goal. Since processes for this type of offender typically include "giving up," treatment should focus on identifying those cognitive distortions that allowed the offender to violate his avoidance goals, examining and rehearsing cognitions that support the avoidance goal, and rehearsal of maintaining this goal. In addition, at this phase, cognitive dissonance (between goals and offense-supportive cognitions and behavior) is introduced and resolved in favor of avoidance of offending. Because these offenders typically demonstrate the tendency to lose control and to "give up" when confronted a situation that places them at risk for offending, motivational enhancement strategies and enhancing self-efficacy expectations may also assist this type of client in preventing future offending. Caution is warranted here, in that self-efficacy should not be enhanced until offense-avoidance skills are effectively developed and have become part of the individual's repertoire and regular functioning. This is because an increase in efficacy expectations without the development of concomitant skills can place the individual at higher risk to re-offend. Finally, treatment focuses on developing skills to prevent loss of control.

Treatment then considers the post-offense evaluation phases, including the individual's affective states and reinforcement immediately following offending (Phase 8) and the impact of this on future goals with respect to offending (Phase 9). Offenders following the avoidant-passive pathway to offending typically experience negative emotional states, such as shame, and attribute the cause of offending to uncontrollable and stable internal factors and states. In treatment the focus is on reinforcing the avoidance goal and developing strategies to cope with loss of control, mis-regulation of emotional states, and so forth, as described above (Phases 2 though 4). One of the great advantages of a GLM-SRM approach is that it primarily works through improving offenders' capacities to function as reflective agents. That is, it helps them to evaluate their lives in terms of what it is they are seeking and whether or not these are worthwhile goals. In this respect, rehabilitation is an evaluative and capacity building process.

Treatment at this stage also reinforces the individual's post-offense commitment to refrain from offending. If there is an indication that the individual has begun to adopt an *offending approach* goal, treatment creates dissonance between processes associated with this goal and the primary goal of avoidance, reinforcing the latter. Of course, this only applies to approach goals directly associated with offending, as the inclusion of adaptive approach goals plays an important role in rehabilitation. Finally, although these offenders typically experience negative affect following the commission of the offense, the experience of positive affect or reinforcement of offending behavior may also occur. For example, the individual may experience sexual gratification or temporary alleviation of loneliness or feelings of low self-worth. Such post-offense experiences are integrated into treatment in a manner that places emphasis on achieving such positive states via appropriate means, to develop the understanding that the alleviation of these states is temporary, to resolve issues that lead to the negative states, to shift the balance of reinforcement contingencies from the positive to the negative consequences associated with the post-offense phase, and to develop strategies that are more effective over the long-term in the alleviation of chronic negative affect.

If treatment is provided in a prison setting, the skills development exercises will be primarily conducted using *in vivo* exercises, such as role-play activities. If provided in the community, the offender can also utilize and practice new skills in actual situations as these arise. However, cognitive reconstruction activities may be effectively developed and reinforced in prison or inpatient settings. Follow-up maintenance treatment and supervision of offenders following an avoidant-passive pathway focuses on maintaining and further entrenching skills in the individual's cognitive and behavioral repertoire, and assisting him to continue to work toward his good lives goals. As the individual is likely to confront failure experiences in real-world situations, he will need to deconstruct these experiences, examining how he may have experienced a lack of control and the reasons for which he did not make use of self-regulation skills. In these cases, treatment may need to revisit skills acquisition and coping strategies, revise the risk management/self-regulation plan, or adjust the good lives plan. If these plans are adjusted, it is essential that the therapist ensure that the plans remain realistic and that the revised plans reflect risk management needs and good lives goals.

Finally, supervision of offenders following the avoidant-passive pathway should involve monitoring of goal achievement, affective states, problem-solving, situations that place them at risk to re-offend, effective implementation of coping strategies, and access to victims within their preferred target group. Any indication that they are losing control or failing to cope should trigger re-assessment and increased intervention and/or supervision.

Treatment of Offenders following the Avoidant-active Pathway

The avoidant-active pathway is a mis-regulation pathway, in which the individual desires to avoid sexual offending (an inhibitory goal) and actively implements strategies to refrain from offending. Because these individuals typically expect that their strategies will be effective, they are able to plan, monitor, and evaluate their behavior.

They usually have adequate self-regulation capacities and have the capabilities to achieve the primary good of autonomy. The strategies they employ, however, are ineffective in preventing offending behavior and may, in fact, paradoxically place them at increased risk to offend. These limitations result from inadequate knowledge of the contingencies associated with certain ways of achieving goals, particularly the goal of not sexually offending. Thus, the primary good of knowledge is often not achieved. For example, an individual who uses alcohol to cope with negative emotional states associated with the desire to offend may increase risk via its disinhibiting effects. Similarly, an offender who masturbates to deviant sexual fantasies as an alternative to acting on these fantasies actually increases his risk to offend via the pairing of deviant arousal and sexual gratification, and the reinforcement and entrenchment of this pairing. In both of these examples, there is a demonstrated lack of knowledge concerning the effects of such choices on their ability to successfully resist the urge to commit a sexual offense.

When individuals following an avoidant-active pathway are confronted with a situation that triggers the desire to offend, they experience negative affect associated with this desire (e.g., anxiety), recognize its incongruence with goals, and make the decision to implement strategies to avoid offending. These offenders typically have high efficacy expectations regarding the effectiveness of the strategies chosen. When the chosen strategies prove ineffective in controlling the desire to offend, the individual then experiences a loss of control, feelings of inadequacy, and decreased self-efficacy. The avoidance goal is then undermined via the interpretation of events and behavior in a concrete manner (cognitive deconstruction). That is, the offender attends to stimuli that support the continuance of offense-related behavior, and begins to use cognitive distortions to justify his actions. These individuals may also experience positive emotional states in addition to negative affective states associated with offending, which can serve to facilitate cognitive distortions that allow offending to occur.

Following the commission of the offense, these individuals typically experience additional negative emotional states, such as guilt, as well as cognitive dissonance associated with the inability to control behavior. Like offenders following the avoidant-passive pathway, offenders following the avoidant-active pathway are likely to evaluate the sexual offense as a negative event, and to make commitments after the offense to reinforce their avoidant goal in the future. However, because the skills used to achieve this goal remain ineffective, they are at risk to commit another sexual offense. These individuals may also conclude that they lack the requisite skills to avoid offending and may subsequently adopt an approach goal in later offenses.

The first steps in treatment with offenders following the avoidant-active pathway are similar to those of the avoidant-passive pathway, and include examining factors that make them vulnerable to offending (Phase 1), identification of situations that initiate the offense progression, analysis of the individual's interpretations of these events based on his core beliefs, and gaining an understanding of the specific nature of the desire for offense-related behaviors (Phase 2). A case formulation is constructed that reflects the relationship between life events, dynamic risk factors, and the offender's basic commitments (primary human goods and their instrumental goods). Treatment also reinforces and validates the individual's goals with respect to offending (i.e., avoidance; Phase 3), and seeks to build into his subsequent lifestyle a suite of personally meaningful and socially acceptable goods. Therapy then seeks to equip the individual with the internal and external conditions required to implement a treatment plan encompassing one or two overarching goods and the lifestyle that is likely to support the achievement of these goods.

For individuals following this pathway, the primary focus of treatment is on the strategies selected to achieve the goal of avoiding offending (Phase 4), which have, in the past, been ineffective, and the implementation of their lifestyle plan (i.e., a good lives plan). Treatment at this phase assists the offender to develop an understanding of the manner in which his attempts to avoid offending have been ineffective and the reasons why these strategies have been ineffective in achieving this goal (i.e., mis-regulation). Where applicable, the manner in which his typical strategies are likely to increase risk is also addressed. This therapeutic tactic seeks to obviate the offender's lack of knowledge, and to equip him with a range of more effective information-gathering and evaluation skills. Treatment then aims to assist the individual to generate strategies that would have been effective in preventing offending, and to subsequently rehearse and entrench these strategies. Treatment also seeks to extinguish the individual's ineffective strategies. Such strategies may be ineffective due to a lack of relevant knowledge about the consequences of engaging in the particular behavior or as a result of problems acquiring important human goods in other life domains. The failure to achieve such goods can lead to frustration, a lack of fulfillment, further problematic life events and, thus, can indirectly result in sexual offending. Simultaneously, treatment would assist in the development and reinforcement of strategies to meet appropriate needs in an acceptable manner – that is, to secure human goods in a manner that is fulfilling and meaningful to the individual. Since these individuals desire to avoid offending, developing an understanding of the victim's experience (perspective-taking/empathy) and entrenching this understanding is also part of the treatment strategy with these offenders, with the aim of inhibiting cognitive distortions that are facilitated via perspective-taking deficits. Similar to the avoidant-passive pathway, it is noted that offenders following the avoidant-active pathway are likely have at least a rudimentary understanding of the victim's experience, given that they attempt to control their behavior and to avoid offending.

While offenders allocated to this pathway tend to have quite good general coping skills, there may be significant problems in some life domains that indirectly cause sexual offending. For example, conflict between the goods of relationships and work achievement could result in feelings of tension and discomfort. This in turn, might cause arguments and discord in a relationship, and may create a cascading sequence of events that culminates in relationship loss, resentment, substance abuse, and offending. Treatment plans should incorporate such insights and be designed to give individuals the capabilities and resources they require to: (a) achieve a better balance in their lives; and (b) greater problem-solving and knowledge generating skills in order to prevent them from utilizing counterproductive "solutions" to their various life stresses.

Next, treatment assists the individual to understand that, when faced with a high risk situation, the implementation of ineffective strategies results in negative emotional states, such as anxiety, the awareness of impending goal failure, loss of control, and lowered self-efficacy expectations (Phases 5 and 6). In turn, this results in abandoning the avoidance goal, adopting an approach goal, and subsequently, offending (Phase 7). By explicitly building access to the various goods likely to meet his needs into an offender's subsequent lifestyle, it is expected that his ability to resist the desire to sexually offend will be increased. In part, this will reflect the fact that the goods indirectly associated with his offending behavior are more likely to be secured and, therefore, the danger of a negative cascade is lessened.

Treatment also considers the post-offense evaluation phases, including the individual's affective states and reinforcement immediately following offending (Phase 8) and the impact of this on future goals with respect to offending (Phase 9). Offenders following the avoidant-active pathway typically experience negative emotional states, such as guilt and anger, as a consequence of their perceived weaknesses and failure to prevent offending. They may blame the victim for this failure, may regard the offense as an aberration caused by the victim, and may renew their commitment to avoid offending in the future. These offenders may also experience positive affect and/or reinforcement of offending behavior. For example, the individual may experience sexual gratification or temporary alleviation of negative states, such as loneliness or feelings of low self-worth, associated with offending. Such post-offense experiences are integrated into treatment in a manner that places emphasis on achieving positive states via appropriate means (related to a wide range of primary goods), to develop the understanding that the alleviation of these states is temporary, to resolve issues that lead to negative affective states, to shift the balance of reinforcement contingencies from the positive to the negative consequences associated with the post-offense phase, and to develop strategies that are more effective over the long-term in the alleviation of chronic negative affect. Each of the above experiences are integrated in treatment with skills deficits and the acquisition of new skills, as well as reinforcing the avoidance goal and developing strategies to cope with the sense of guilt and failure, as described above (Phases 2 though 4). If there is indication that the individual has begun to adopt an offending approach goal, treatment creates dissonance between processes associated with this goal and the primary goal of avoidance of offending, reinforcing the latter.

If treatment is provided in a prison setting, the skills development exercises will be primarily conducted using *in vivo* exercises, such as role-play activities. If provided in the community, the offender can also utilize and practice new skills in actual situations that arise. However, cognitive reconstruction activities may be effectively developed and reinforced in prison or inpatient settings. Follow-up maintenance treatment and supervision of offenders following an avoidant-active pathway focuses on maintaining goals and entrenching new strategies in the individual's cognitive and behavioral repertoire. As the individual is likely to experience failure in real-world situations, he will need to deconstruct these experiences and examine where he may have relied on his previous, ineffective strategies. In these cases, treatment may need to revisit the newly developed strategies, revise the self-regulation plan, or adjust the good lives plan. If these plans are adjusted, it is essential that the therapist ensure that the plans remain realistic, and that the revised plans reflect risk management needs and good lives goals.

Finally, supervision of offenders following the avoidant-active pathway should monitor affective states, problem-solving, situations that place the offender at risk to re-offend, the implementation of effective strategies, and access to victims within the offender's preferred target group. Supervision should also assist him to continue to work toward his good lives goals. It will also involve implementing and monitoring a lifestyle plan that reflects the individual's important goals and underlying commitments (i.e., primary goods) that were developed during treatment. Any indication that the offender is relying on previous ineffective strategies, or is engaging in victim-blaming or other similar cognitive distortions, should trigger re-assessment alongside increased intervention and supervision.

Treatment of Offenders Following the Approach-automatic Pathway

The approach-automatic pathway is an under-regulation or disinhibition pathway characterized by an acquisitional or appetitive goal, and impulsivity in offending behavior. Individuals following this pathway fail to control their behavior, and respond relatively rapidly to situational cues on the basis of well-entrenched cognitive and behavioral scripts that support and facilitate sexual offending. These individuals do not attempt to refrain from offending, but rather act to ensure their needs are met, albeit in an impulsive or unregulated manner. As such, these individuals have approach goals with respect to offending, and planning is relatively rudimentary and unsophisticated. Furthermore, it is likely that they lack interest in the needs of others or experience periodic disruptions to their functioning that overrides such interests (e.g., periods of anger, intoxication, etc.). Goals and strategies (and their activation) are also unlikely to be under the immediate attentional control of the offender, as they are activated rapidly as a function of *long-standing* scripts and responses in the individual's behavioral repertoire. The fact that individuals allocated to this pathway find it hard to set goals, plan, and to evaluate and implement such plans points to their consistent inability to achieve the good of autonomy. That is, they are unable to reflect in a systematic way on what is in their best interests and to develop a set of strategies that is likely to promote such interests while avoiding harm to themselves and others.

When individuals following an approach-automatic pathway experience an event that triggers the desire to offend or that places them at risk to offend, they exhibit a lack of restraint and may experience either positive or negative emotional states. Positive emotional states, which may be more likely to occur, result from anticipation of achieving *one's goal*, indicate satisfactory progression toward the goal, and (following the commission of the offense) are associated with success and gratification. In addition, this "success" leads to further reinforcement of offending behavior, increasing the likelihood of future offending. It is important to note that "success" at achieving goals may ultimately result in further harm to themselves because the primary human goods associated with these goals are unlikely to be secured. Thus, the means (instrumental goods) upon which this type of offender relies to achieve his approach goals are inappropriate. This may be because they lack knowledge of what is the most effective way to achieve valued outcomes, because they lack the capabilities, resources, or opportunities to secure them, or because they have learned throughout their lives to secure these goods via offensive behavior.

As indicated above, offending is triggered by situational cures that activate well-entrenched beliefs and scripts for individuals following the approach-automatic pathway. Common cognitive scripts for these offenders include a sense of sexual or other entitlement, hostile or stereotyped attitudes (e.g., toward women), general hostility or suspiciousness, or beliefs that sexual activity with children is acceptable. Considerable cognitive distortions, which justify and excuse offending, are evident.

As indicated in Volume I, the predominant issues to be addressed in treatment among offenders following the approach-automatic pathway include raising awareness, altering over-learned cognitive and behavioral scripts, resolving issues that form the foundation of these scripts (e.g., the causes of a hostile or suspicious worldview), and changing offense-related goals. The latter refers to deciding not to offend, the identification of the basic goods that their offending reveals are important to them, as well as finding alternative ways of achieving such experiences. In increasing awareness, treatment aims to assist the offender to understand the attitudes and scripts he possesses, their origin, the manner in he responds impulsively to stimuli in the environment, and the manner in which he interprets these stimuli based on identified scripts. From a GLM perspective, scripts are the basic beliefs, attitudes, and strategies that underpin the different aspects of a person's lifestyle. Scripts structure the manner by which events are interpreted by individuals and tend to be so entrenched within individuals' everyday lives that they are rarely noticed. Treatment has the fundamental goal of altering these attitudes and scripts for offenders following this pathway.

One particular focus of treatment is on assisting the offender to achieve meta-cognitive control — that is, to acquire the ability to reflect on their interests, beliefs, desires, and needs, and the degree to which their actions promote or hinder these. In addition to addressing reliance on scripts, treatment aims to assist the individual in achieving functional self-regulation, including learning new cognitive and behavioral responses to environmental stimuli. Finally, treatment targets approach goals with respect to offending in an effort to develop avoidance goals to replace approach goals. This change flows naturally from positive changes in attitudes and their attendant cognitive scripts. All of these interventions are designed to enhance the autonomous functioning of offenders following an approach-automatic pathway.

The first steps in treatment with offenders following the approach-automatic pathway are similar to those described above, and include examining factors that make them vulnerable to offending (Phase I), identifying situations that initiate the offense progression, analyzing interpretations of these events based on core beliefs and offense-related goals, and understanding the specific nature of the desire for offense-related behaviors (Phase 2). Unlike the avoidance pathways, however, treatment does not reinforce and validate the individual's goals with respect to offending (Phase 3), but rather assists the individual to understand the development of these goals, to question these goals in light of life goals and social norms, to consider alternative goals, and to evaluate the potential positive impact of the latter on the individual's life.

In raising awareness with respect to longstanding factors (Phase 1), treatment assists the individual to examine developmental and life events that have led to the formation of an approach goal, offense-supportive attitudes, and cognitive and behavioral scripts. As considerable cognitive dissonance is likely to be introduced, the individual is likely to become defensive and, as such, methods such as Socratic questioning (Beck, 1995; Beck et al., 1979; Newman, 2003), presenting "neutral" information, and contextualizing change within the offender's own personal and life goals may be the most successful methods in initiating consideration of change and cognitive restructuring, particularly during the early stages of treatment. It is important that therapists are aware that the individual is being asked to change long-standing goals, beliefs, and patterns of cognition and behavior. The therapist must proceed accordingly, changing intervention styles when resistance is encountered. The fact that such individuals typically have not reflected on their behavior means that aspects of their sexually abusive actions (e.g., motives, goods sought, etc.) may be quite unintelligible to them.

Treatment then proceeds to examination of the individual's desire for offensive sexual activities (Phase 2) and his goals with respect to offending (Phase 3). Treatment assists the individual to understand precisely what needs he is attempting to meet (e.g., sexual, intimate, retribution, etc.) and deconstructs the offense goal. This process enables him to identify core needs that are being met through offending – that is, the primary goods that are being sought and the means employed to achieve them. The manner in which treatment proceeds next depends upon the needs the individual is attempting to meet. Specifically, if the individual is attempting to meet appropriate goals, such as sexual or intimacy needs, treatment proceeds with the examination of appropriate means by which the offender can meet this goal and by targeting the individual's inadequate self-regulation. If the individual is attempting to meet goals such as retribution or the expression of anger based on well-entrenched hostility, treatment must resolve these issues prior to targeting self-regulation deficits. One way of doing this is to enquire exactly what goods underlie such reactions. In our experience, grievance related concerns frequently reflect a sense of injustice (i.e., good of community and fairness) or autonomy issues (i.e., the sense that others are attempting to unreasonably dominate or dismiss one's value as a person). The goal at this stage is for the offender to examine and abandon these views and offense-supportive beliefs so that he may later respond differently to similar situations in future (i.e., cognitive restructuring). This is made easier if the origin of such reactions has been elucidated. Then the primary good can be explicitly targeted in a way that is more likely to result in enhanced autonomy (or a sense of independence). This example rather nicely illustrates the added value of the GLM to the treatment of sexual offenders. The risk factor of inappropriate anger or suspicion/hostility is treated as a red flag indicating a problem in the way certain kinds of human goods are sought. A careful analysis of the individual's offense process and relevant background details reveals the source of this problematic worldview. The therapist can then ensure that access to the relevant good is possible through the establishment of opportunities and capabilities relevant to the person concerned. Thus an avoidance goal (e.g., modifying anger, decreasing hostility) is replaced by an approach goal that is inconsistent with offending. The offender is equipped with the skills to function independently, to establish relationships characterized by reciprocity, and to interpret the behavior of others differently (in a manner that is not suspicious).

Once the individual's goal has been delineated and resolved, the next step in treatment is to examine offense planning, selection of offense strategies, and responses when encountering situations that place him at risk to offend (Phases 4 through 7). However, given that planning is relatively rudimentary and the individual tends to offend impulsively, the focus at this stage of treatment with offenders following the approach-automatic pathway is to address impulsivity and under-regulation. In doing so, treatment focuses on deconstructing offense and offense-related experiences to determine the individual's perceptions of these experiences, the manner in which he interprets these experiences, and the core beliefs and scripts that are activated by the experience and its interpretation. As these have typically been outside the offender's attentional control, treatment delineates this process in a step-by-step process in order to assist him to understand that he undertook decisions throughout the offense progression. Self-monitoring techniques and exercises (Heidt & Marx, 2003; Leahy, 2001) may be particularly useful to achieve this treatment goal with this group of offenders.

Treatment then assists the individual to learn and rehearse meta-cognitive techniques (Wells, 2000; Wells & Matthews, 1994, 1996) consistent with new treatment goals, which function to entrench new cognitive and behavioral response scripts. For example, the offender for whom a particular situation triggers anger (which has previously led to offending) learns to monitor these situations, to identify when he is responding with anger to that situation, to interpret the situation differently, and to implement an alternative, non-offending response. This alternative response includes thinking in a different manner with respect to the event as well as responding cognitively and behaviorally in a different manner. Using the example of anger, the individual may be encouraged to think, *"I will not let her provoke me. I am not going to give her the power to make me angry and send me pack to prison"*, rather than, *"She is provoking me.... I will show her she can't do that... I'll teach her a lesson"*.

In addition to the above, offenders following the approach-automatic pathway may benefit from developing an understanding of the victim's experience (perspective-taking/empathy) and entrenching this understanding, as a mechanism by which offending and offense-related cognition and behavior can be inhibited. It is essential that cognitions associated with such an understanding are rehearsed and entrenched as an immediate response to situations that trigger the desire to offend for offenders following this pathway.

Treatment also considers the post-offense evaluation phases, including the individual's affective states and further entrenchment of cognitive and behavioral scripts via reinforcement (Phase 8) and the impact of this on future goals with respect to offending (Phase 9). Offenders following the approach-automatic pathway typically experience positive emotional states as a result of success in achieving their goal. They are likely to blame the victim via attributing responsibility for provocation of the offense. These experiences are integrated into the treatment change strategy as described above (Phases 2 though 4). The aim is to shift the balance of reinforcement contingencies from the positive to the negative consequences associated with the post-offense phase.

Treatment effectiveness with offenders following the approach-automatic pathway can be enhanced via shaping and the use of positive reinforcement for successive approximations of an avoidant goal with respect to offending, for evidence of changes in core beliefs and scripts, and improvements in meta-cognitive capacity and skills (Wells, 2000; Wells & Matthews, 1994, 1996). Since a major goal of treatment with this offender group is to increase awareness, indications of improved awareness on the part of the offender must be reinforced by treatment providers, even if the change is slight. Reinforcement of successive approximations is essential to treatment change for offenders following this pathway. Offenders following this pathway will also require considerable rehearsal to develop and come to rely upon new (non-offending) scripts and behaviors.

It is imperative that a good lives plan for altering the offender's future lifestyle is used to guide these interventions. Without this plan, the focus of treatment will be on generating a list of risk factors and deficits without offering the person incentives for changing his behavior. It is likely that offenders obtain certain benefits from offending, and it is only reasonable to expect them to change their behavior if they are offered alternative ways of securing these desired outcomes. Such incentives will also function to increase engagement with the treatment process on the part of the offender. Of course, from the perspective of the GLM, it is necessary to trace the relationship between the individual's desires and basic human goods. Typically, it is a question of increasing his awareness of the types of goals/goods that his offending indicates are important to him (a bit like linking automatic thoughts in depression to underlying dysfunctional core beliefs) and how his lifestyle at the time of his sexual crimes failed to provide him with personally meaningful ways of securing these goods. This will automatically increase the offender's level of motivation and create a bridge between treatment and his life (i.e., promoting goods and reducing risk).

Since much of treatment for offenders following this pathway focuses on awareness-raising and cognitive change, the opportunity exists to develop new skills, such as meta-cognition (Wells, 2000; Wells & Matthews, 1994, 1996), in both prison and community settings. Situations to which the individual responds impulsively are likely to arise in either setting, and are utilized in treatment to raise awareness and to effect cognitive and behavioral change. Follow-up maintenance treatment and supervision of offenders following an approach-automatic pathway focuses on maintaining the new offense goal (i.e., avoidance), on reinforcing this goal, and on the generation of new cognitive schema and behavioral strategies. As the individual is likely to experience failure in real-world situations, he will need to deconstruct these experiences and examine where he may have regressed to reliance on previous offense-supportive scripts or where he may have responded impulsively. In these cases, treatment may need to revisit the newly developed strategies and increase monitoring, as well as re-visit the individual's good lives plan in order to ensure it is achievable and that the any changes to these plans continue to reflect risk management needs.

Finally, supervision of offenders following the approach-automatic pathway should involve monitoring of cognitive schema via the offender's verbalizations of beliefs and responses to situations as these arise, including both situations that place the offender at risk to re-offend and other, more general situations. Supervision should also monitor access to victims within the offender's preferred target group. This offender is likely to benefit from strong external and community support systems. Any indication that the offender is relying on previous offense-supportive cognitive scripts, is responding impulsively, or is not achieving his good lives goals should trigger re-assessment alongside increased intervention and supervision.

Treatment of Offenders following the Approach-Explicit Pathway

The approach-explicit pathway is characterized by intact self-regulation. Offenders following this pathway consciously and explicitly plan their offenses, and have well-developed strategies to achieve this acquisitional goal. The fundamental goals held by the offender are higher-level ones designed to meet needs, such as personal power, intimacy, or control. Belief systems within this pathway explicitly support sexual offending, such as through attitudes sustaining sexual activity with children or hostile attitudes toward women, and behavior is not disinhibited or misregulated. There is a direct route between some of the primary goods individuals hold and their offending behavior. For example, individuals may seek the good of intimacy through sex with a child or the good of autonomy through the inappropriate sexual domination of an adult. The fact that offenders lack the necessary internal (i.e., capabilities, attitudes) and external (i.e., opportunities, supports, resources) means to achieve these goods in personally meaningful and socially acceptable ways means that they are more likely to engage in dysfunctional behaviors to achieve them.

Individuals following an approach-explicit pathway may experience an event that triggers a desire to offend, placing them at risk to offend, or they may create the opportunity to offend. The desire to offend might be either associated with the expression of negative emotional states (e.g., expressing anger through aggression), core beliefs, or the acquisition of positive emotional states or sexual gratification via offending. Offending is viewed as an acceptable means to achieve these goals, and the offender does not attempt to avoid offending. Positive emotional states, which are more likely to occur than negative affect, result from anticipation of achieving one's goal.

Recall that primary human goods represent the most fundamental level of personal goals, and that instrumental goods are ways of achieving these fundamental goods. The goals that approach-explicit offenders seek through sexually abusive behavior are usefully viewed as activities expected to lead to the primary human goods. Of course, for most offenders this does not occur and the individual is left only partially satisfied. For example, seeking a sense of personal power through controlling another person will not actually help an individual to achieve true autonomy. The types of primary goods sought are likely to vary among approach-explicit offenders and will not always be (sexual) pleasure. In our research on the offense process, we have noted that offenders try to find diverse outcomes through abusive sex, ranging from intimacy to emotional control (Ward et al., 2004). To reiterate, the presence of an approach goal toward sexual offending indicates merely that there is a direct route between primary human goods and sexual crimes; what really matters from a clinical perspective is the type of primary good being sought. Thus approach goals in both of the approach pathways function as markers for more fundamental goals such as autonomy, relatedness or play (i.e., primary goods).

Further, positive affect serves to indicate satisfactory progression toward the goal in question, perhaps heightening the desire to offend throughout the offense progression. Following the commission of the offense, these individuals typically experience positive emotional states as a result of experiencing success in achieving their goal. Offending behavior is reinforced, and these offenders may learn from their behavior in such a manner as to refine future offense strategies.

They may display real expertise in the commission of an offense, and may refine and enhance their offending related skills as their criminal history progresses.

Common cognitive scripts for offenders following the approach-explicit pathway include a strong sense of sexual entitlement, hostile or stereotyped attitudes toward a specific group of individuals or toward the world in general, or beliefs that the sexual abuse or aggression is acceptable. The individual may or may not engage in cognitive distortions to justify and excuse offending, as they believe that their behavior is acceptable and therefore does not require justification.

The focus of treatment for offenders following the approach-explicit pathway includes changing goals with respect to offending behavior. Of course, this requires understanding exactly what benefits or higher level goals the individual seeks via sexual offending and ascertaining what capabilities, resources, and opportunities individuals require to achieve socially acceptable valued outcomes. As indicated in Volume I, the core beliefs of these offenders typically relate either to beliefs concerning the self and intimacy with others, or to a sense of having been unfairly treated or wronged. The former set of beliefs are more likely to be associated with positive affect, while the latter are more likely to be associated with negative affect. A sense of entitlement may also be evident, as may nonsexual offending behavior. The key point is that the primary goods sought by offenders will be associated with a set of beliefs and attitudes that specify the significance of the outcome sought and the steps required to achieve it. Beliefs are always in the service of values and inform individuals how, when, and why certain steps are necessary to achieve their desires (Ward, Vess, Gannon, & Collie, in press).

Treatment of these offenders differs significantly from individuals following other pathways, particularly the avoidance-based pathways. The first step in treatment involves establishing a therapeutic atmosphere conducive to the disclosure of intentional harmful behavior, and the development of this tendency. It is typically unnecessary to ensure that treatment is conducive to disclosure of self-protective mechanisms, as the typical approach-explicit offender does not engage in these types of mechanisms. Rather, the offender needs to be encouraged, through motivational enhancement techniques (Levensky, 2003; Miller & Rollnick, 1991; Miller, Zweben, & DiClemente, 1992), to report on offensive beliefs, attitudes, and sexually deviant cognition and behavior, about which he may not be forthcoming. As these offenders are unlikely to regard their behavior as problematic, techniques for individuals at the precontemplative stage of change (DiClemente, 1991; Prochaska & DiClemente, 1982, 1986), such as awareness raising, are most likely to be the most effective at this early stage in treatment. In addition, as a strategy to engage these offenders in treatment, treatment takes an approach by which offenders are encouraged to work toward their goals and to act in their own interests (although obviously with respect to pro-social goals and behavior only). The therapist stresses that the primary human good that is of most importance to the offender and appears to be motivating his abusive behavior (e.g., intimacy) is acceptable. The problem resides in the way the offender sets out to secure it. This has the advantage of retaining valued aspects of the offenders' life, upon which they often base their identities (e.g., achievement, etc.), while at the same time encouraging them to think of other ways they can achieve this outcome.

We would like to make our position more concrete by discussing two examples of the link between identities and offending from our own clinical experience. One of us worked with a man who obtained enormous satisfaction from teaching and shaping his step-daughter's personality and behavior. He saw himself as a psychological architect who literally designed and created his step-daughter. The goods of mastery, creativity, and autonomy were directly associated with this domination, which ultimately led to his sexual offending. Another example concerns a man who sought relatedness and intimacy with vulnerable children. He saw himself as a caring, giving, and loving individual who could heal distressed and abused children. The goods of relatedness and mastery were directly involved and the image of himself as a kind of social worker was causally implicated in his sexually abusive behavior. In both of these examples, the pursuit of primary goods in dysfunctional ways was linked to the men's identities. The successful management and treatment of both these men would be greatly facilitated by accepting the importance of their primary goods and associated personal identities, but finding more socially acceptable ways of realizing them. For example, this could be achieved by providing alternative ways of caring for others (adults) and outlets for the need to teach and train other people.

Treatment of offenders following the approach-explicit pathway begins with the examination of developmental and historical events that have led to well-entrenched attitudes that support offending and associated goals, such as retribution or entitlement (Phase 1). The offender is assisted to examine, in detail, those circumstances that ultimately led to goals that support sexual offending and, if relevant, other offending behavior. The desire for deviant sexual behavior and the explicit intention to offend (Phases 2 and 3) are also examined. Treatment assists the individual to understand precisely what needs he is attempting to meet (e.g., autonomy, perhaps through retribution for a perceived slight or insult) and deconstructs the offense goal. This process enables to individual to identify core needs that are being met through offending. The aim of treatment at these phases is to enable the offender to identify the association between these early experiences, to motivate him to contemplate the notion that he can achieve his goals via other, non-offending, methods, and to instill the idea that offending may impede his other life goals (i.e., appealing to the offender's sense of self-interest). One of the real advantages of using the GLM to enrich treatment of sexual offenders is that it directly appeals to self-interest in a way that serves to increase individuals' motivation to engage in the challenging process of behavior change while not entrenching narrow and selfish attitudes. It does this by directly appealing to an offender's overarching primary good and ways of living that promote this primary good, and helping to consolidate a more adaptive personal identity. As such, this model may be particularly useful for offenders following the approach-explicit pathway.

When the offender is able to identify these attitudes and their origins, treatment then assists him to identify overall life goals and to consider the manner in which offending defeats these goals. It does this by drawing from the GLM and constructing a treatment plan that builds the various primary goods into a different type of lifestyle – one that is personally meaningful and satisfying to the individual and at the same time is ethically and legally acceptable.

In examining the selection of strategies and the commission of the sexual offense (Phases 4 though 7), offenders who experience predominantly positive affect are challenged to determine other, non-offending ways to achieve these same states. The primary aim of treatment is to eliminate the need to achieve these states via attitude change or to meet these needs in a non-abusive manner. For example, for the offender who seeks to obtain a sense of personal power and control via offending, treatment aims to examine the basis of this need, to eliminate it through resolution of issues leading to that need, and to uncover the primary goal he seeks. Furthermore, it is essential that the primary goods associated with these issues are secured via other means. This requires therapists to carefully consider the offenders' abilities, interests, and external circumstances and to assist him to develop the capabilities and opportunities that are necessary to satisfy them. Attitudes and cognitive distortions that suggest achieving power over others is acceptable are targeted for change, and alternative, socially acceptable sources of personal power and equitability in relationships are instilled. In examining the selection of strategies and the commission of the sexual offense among offenders who experience predominantly negative affect (Phases 4 though 7), treatment aims to change the offender's need driving his offending or to develop appropriate ways to meet this need, as appropriate to the particular case. For example, treatment aims to resolve the core issues surrounding a sense of having been unfairly treated or wronged and assists him to overcome these sentiments. Therapy then examines the offending process to demonstrate the manner in which offending meets this need, and assists the offender to find other ways to meet these needs. As such, in analyzing the offense precursors and progression, the principal aim of treatment is to resolve the need for the offensive behavior at its origin, to change concomitant attitudes and cognitive distortions, and to reduce the sense of entitlement typically demonstrated by these offenders. The source of these attitudes may vary depending on the type of primary goods that are evident in an individual's offense process and his own personal history. For some, it could be entitlement relating to appreciation (mastery goals), while for others, the expectation that they are entitled to love and acceptance (relatedness goals).

In examining the final phases of the offense progression (Phases 8 and 9), treatment aims to raise awareness of negative experiences or affect, if these exist, that may have arisen for the offender in addition to the predominant positive emotional states. In this case, treatment aims to shift the balance from a focus on positive experiences to a focus on negative outcomes of offensive behavior, and assists the offender to determine other, non-offending methods by which he can achieve positive states that do not result in negative outcomes and harm to others. For example, the offender may have experienced sexual gratification or positive affect as a result of having successfully sought retribution, as well as fear of detection. The offender is assisted to come to the realization that not offending allows him to avoid fear of detection. At this stage, if treatment has successfully begun to resolve the core issues that lead to offending, it will be easier to shift this balance.

Once attitude change has begun and pro-social goals are set, treatment then assists the individual to learn and rehearse meta-cognitive techniques (Wells, 2000; Wells & Matthews, 1994, 1996) consistent with new treatment goals, and to entrench new cognitive and behavioral response scripts. For example, the offender who experiences a need for retribution in a particular situation which has previously led to offending learns to manage this need for retribution via cognitive restructuring and reiteration of pro-social goals (as being in his own best interest). This alternative response includes both thinking differently with respect to the event, as well as responding behaviorally in a different manner. Using the example of retribution, the individual may be encouraged to think, *"I will not let myself be provoked, it is not worth the trouble. I will be the superior person if I just leave this situation"; "What is it that I am really looking for here? Is it love, praise, or acknowledgement? How else can I achieve these important goals"?*

Treatment effectiveness can be enhanced with offenders following the approach-explicit pathway via shaping and the use of positive reinforcement for successive approximations of honest disclosure, attitude change, and changes to core beliefs and scripts, and positive movement toward appropriate acquisition of primary goods. As a major goal of treatment with this offender is to increase awareness, indications of increasing awareness on the part of the offender are reinforced by treatment providers. Offenders following this pathway will require considerable rehearsal to entrench new scripts and behaviors, and to abandon former pro-offending scripts and attitudes.

As much of treatment for offenders following this pathway focuses on awareness-raising and cognitive change, the opportunity exists to develop new skills, such as meta-cognition (Wells, 2000; Wells & Matthews, 1994, 1996), in both prison and community settings. Situations to which the individual responds in an antisocial manner are likely to arise in either setting, and can be utilized in treatment to raise awareness and to effect attitudinal, cognitive, and behavioral change. Follow-up maintenance treatment and supervision of offenders following an approach-explicit pathway focuses on maintaining attitude change, avoidance of offending, continued honest disclosure, reinforcement of positive changes, and continued progress in the appropriate acquisition of primary goods and achievement of life goals. A particular focus is on continuing to entrench new, non-offending attitudes, cognitive schema, and behavioral strategies in the individual's repertoire, and reinforcing these positive changes. As the individual is likely to experience failure in real-world situations, he will need to deconstruct these experiences and examine where he may have regressed to reliance on previous offense-supportive scripts and cognitive schema. In these cases, treatment may need to revisit the newly developed strategies and increase monitoring, revise the self-regulation plan, or adjust the good lives plan. If these plans are adjusted, it is essential that the therapist ensure that the plans remain realistic and that the revised plans reflect risk management needs and good lives goals.

Finally, supervision of offenders following the approach-explicit pathway should involve considerable monitoring of the individual, particularly for evidence of the re-emergence of previous core problematic issues as well as their associated attitudes and cognitive distortions. These should be assessed via the offender's verbalizations, responses to situations as these arise, and collateral reports. This includes both situations that place the offender at risk to re-offend and other, more general situations. Access to victims within the offender's preferred target group should be avoided and monitored in supervision. This offender is likely to benefit from strong external and community support systems and is a good candidate for a Circle of Support intervention (Wilson & Prinzo, 2001; Wilson, Prinzo, & Picheca, 2003). Any indication that the offender's previous core problematic issues are re-emerging or that the offender is accessing previous offense-supportive cognitive scripts should trigger re-assessment and increased intervention and supervision.

The presence of risk factors function as red flags that valued goals are being threatened, and that the offender should reflect on his life circumstances and seek to make some changes. It is important that the individual looks to reinstall benefits or goods in his life and not simply seek to ignore the high risk elements. Otherwise, there is a real danger that he is simply reopening a route to re-offending.

Summary

This chapter has outlined the application of treatment to each of the four pathways indicated by the self-regulation model of offending, and places specific intervention techniques and methods within both the SRM and GLM models. It is apparent from the above discussion that treatment approach and methods vary as a function of the pathway to offending followed by the individual offender. The preceding discussion also serves to describe the manner in which individuals' overarching life goals are incorporated into the treatment process, and the manner in which the assessment of risk, need, and responsivity of individual offenders is placed within both the treatment process and the theoretical models. Thus treatment is tailored to individuals' good lives goals, the specific pathway to offending followed, and the dynamic risk factors evidenced by the individual, using the effective therapeutic practices described earlier in this volume.

The four chapters which follow apply the SRM (supplemented by the GLM) to the treatment of sexual offenders following the four SRM pathways, respectively. Each chapter utilizes the case examples that illustrate the core features of a particular pathway found in Volume I. It is important to note that this discussion is designed to be illustrative of each sample case. Because the SRM is a flexible model that should take slightly different forms depending on the nature of the problems exhibited by sexual offenders and their underlying causes (Ward et al., 2004; Ward & Gannon, 2006), interventions additional to those noted in the following cases may be appropriate. In addition, offenders following the same pathway will often display different goals, life circumstances, risk levels, offense characteristics, and dynamic risk factors (Yates & Kingston, 2005; Yates et al., 2003). For example, for some individuals, their offending behavior centers around establishing a sense of intimacy with another person, while for others the primary aim could be to assert the need for dominance. Dynamic risk factors will also differ on an individual basis for offenders following the same pathway. A virtue of embedding the SRM within the GLM theory of rehabilitation is that it alerts clinicians to the fact that sexual offenders frequently follow different etiological trajectories. Although treatment must be structured and target criminogenic needs, offenders following different pathways require distinct treatment packages within this structure in order to appropriately target treatment to their goals, risk, criminogenic needs, and responsivity characteristics.

Chapter 5: Treatment Implications for Offenders Following an Avoidant-passive Pathway

Case Example Synopsis

Mr. W has been convicted for two sexual offenses against boys under the age of ten years. A third charge for a similar offense, committed prior to his current conviction, was dismissed. All offenses, which Mr. W committed between the ages of fifteen and twenty-three years, involved fondling and fellatio. Mr. W received a fine and a period of probation for the first offense and a prison term for the second offense. Mr. W has no other criminal history.

Mr. W has a stable family history and supportive parents. Mr. W has never attained a long-term intimate relationship with an adult partner. He reports never having engaged in sexual intercourse with an age-appropriate female and that he is not sexually attracted to adult males. He indicates that he is shy and reluctant to establish age-appropriate relationships.

Mr. W's offenses are based in a variety of skills deficits, including intimacy and social relationships, and sexual arousal to boys. The first two incidents of offending were similar. In the first, he made contact with an unknown prepubescent male whom he manipulated to go to a park. Mr. W then fondled and fellated the victim. The second involved "cruising" his neighborhood to find a victim. He reported that, at that time, he had been unable to find employment and felt worthless. The index offense was committed against a neighbor's child whom he had agreed to baby-sit.

Prior to offending, at the age of twelve, Mr. W began to masturbate to fantasies of boys, although he attempted to think about age-appropriate females while doing so. This strategy ultimately failed, and he felt guilty about his sexual attraction to boys. He spoke to a school counselor following his first offense but reported no impact of this intervention, after which he "just wanted to forget" about the incident. He reports sexual attraction to boys that appears preferential. He has not participated in treatment for sexual offending.

Pathway Allocated: Avoidant-passive

Within the self-regulation model of offending, the avoidant-passive pathway is characterized as an under-regulation pathway, in which the individual desires to avoid sexual offending (an inhibitory goal) but lacks the requisite skills to prevent it. The individual also tends to not actively engage in activities that would prevent offending, or simply attempts to deny urges or to distract himself in order to avoid engaging in the undesired behavior. When these individuals are faced with situations that trigger the desire to offend, they experience a loss of control or disinhibition resulting from negative affective states and a lack of adequate strategies that may be used to achieve the goal of refraining from offending. These individuals are likely to have low self-efficacy expectations about their ability to avoid offending, to experience negative affective states associated with offending behavior, and to covertly, rather than overtly, plan their offenses.

Mr. W is allocated to the approach-avoidant pathway due to his desire to avoid offending (e.g., feeling guilty after the offenses). Although he attempted on occasion to intervene, he generally tended to ignore high risk situations, to view his actions as beyond his control, to feel helpless and inadequate, and to avoid acting to address his problems. His early strategies as an adolescent, prior to offending (i.e., avoidance, switching the object of his masturbatory fantasizes from boys to age-appropriate females), failed. It is noted that Mr. W may be moving toward an avoidant-active pathway as indicated in his third offense, in which he actively sought out a victim by "cruising".

Identified Risk Factors

Prior to treatment, risk factors are identified to evaluate Mr. W's risk for sexual re-offending based on static and dynamic factors. This assessment provides information necessary for treatment matching as well as supervision.

Static Risk Factors.

- Single
- Prior charges/convictions for sexual offenses
- Sexual offenses committed against unrelated victims
- Sexual offenses committed against stranger victims
- Sexual offenses committed against male victims

Actuarial risk assessment measures risk to re-offend relative to other sexual offenders, using static factors empirically demonstrated to be predictive of recidivism. Using actuarial assessment of static risk (Static-99; Hanson & Thornton, 1999), Mr. W's identified risk factors place him at the moderate-high risk to re-offend relative to other sexual offenders. Normative data for offenders falling into this category demonstrate a probability of sexual recidivism of 33%, 38%, and 40% over 5, 10, and 15 years, respectively. Mr. W is young (under 25 years), is a sexual recidivist, and has not maintained an intimate relationship for at least two years. He has also offended against male victims, unrelated victims, and strangers.

Mr. W is unlikely to present a risk for violent or general criminal behavior. He has no history of nonsexual violence or other criminality, nor is there evidence of attitudes supportive of crime or association with pro-criminal family or peers. Mr. W presents as generally pro-social in areas other than his sexual behavior. For example, he does not demonstrate attitudes supportive of sexual offending, and he has stable employment and positive community support from his family.

Dynamic Risk Factors/Treatment Targets. Dynamic risk factors are those factors empirically demonstrated to be predictive of sexual recidivism and that can be changed through intervention. The following treatment targets for Mr. W were based on case-specific factors as assessed against these dynamic risk factors, such as those described within the Stable 2000 (Hanson & Harris, 2004).

- Intimacy/relationship deficits
- Social rejection/loneliness
- Deviant sexual interest/preference
- Attitudes supportive of sexual activity with children
- Problems with general self-regulation (problem-solving, coping with negative emotionality)
- Emotional identification/congruence with children (provisional)
- Use of sex as coping mechanism (provisional)

Mr. W requires intervention in the area of intimate relationships. He admits that he feels uncomfortable with female peers and has experienced difficulty establishing intimate relationships with adult females. He reports that he has not attempted to establish age-appropriate relationships with adult males. Relatedly, Mr. W appears to have difficulty in social relationships generally. The school counselor with whom he met following his first offense recommended that he take action to deal with social isolation and loneliness.

Mr. W's sexual attraction to boys, including sexual arousal and masturbation to fantasies of boys, indicates the presence of deviant sexual interest and likely preference. This is supported by Mr. W's self-reported inability to achieve arousal and ejaculation during fantasy unless the target is a prepubescent male and the failure of attempts to fantasize about age-appropriate females when he was an adolescent. His ability to achieve arousal and sexual gratification with either adult females or adults males is not known. He expresses a lack of interest in adult males, and has attempted to establish relationships with adult females, which he reported failed as a result of his shyness and reluctance with respect to sexual behavior. Because the extent to which Mr. W's offenses are associated with deviant sexual preference is unknown early in the assessment stage, specialized assessment (i.e., phallometric or sexual interest testing) combined with a comprehensive survey of sexual history and interests, is indicated. Results of this assessment will provide information regarding any additional treatment targets and methods for Mr. W.

Mr. W displays cognitive distortions that enable him to engage in sexual behavior with male children. Clearly, during offending or while engaging in sexual fantasy, he employs a cognitive mechanism that allows him to violate his avoidance goal and to ultimately offend, despite his belief that this is wrong. At the assessment stage, it remains unknown precisely what cognitive and affective processes permit Mr. W to engage in behavior that clearly violates his beliefs. It may be the case that, at times when his chronic vulnerability factors are activated (for example when he experiences negative affect such as lack of intimacy or feelings of worthless in a specific situation) he seeks to meet these needs or to counteract these feelings. As such, Mr. W may seek out male children via a series of unplanned steps which allow him to encounter a situation in which he can meet his needs. Once in such a situation, Mr. W lacks the strategies necessary to refrain from acting on his desires, experiences a lack of control, gives in, and abandons his avoidance goal. The role that deviant sexual arousal and/or preference plays in this process, as indicated above, is not yet known at the assessment stage. Mr. W makes statements that are suggestive of possible emotional identification or congruence with children. However, what is unknown is the contribution of (a) feeling comfortable with children (emotional identification/congruence), (b) cognitive distortions that justify the behavior during the offense, and (c) cognitive distortions that reflect core attitudes supportive of sexual offending, to his offending behavior. Thus, the interplay of these factors must be evaluated during treatment, and addressed accordingly.

Finally, it is also possible that Mr. W uses sex as a mechanism to cope with negative emotional states. Specifically, he committed the second incident (for which he was not charged) at a time during which he reported feeling worthless. This was triggered as a result of graduating from university and being unable to find a job. He also reported that when he was feeling lonely and socially isolated, he would go for walks in the park and look at the children. However, the full range of behaviors typically associated with the use of sex as a coping mechanism (e.g., compulsivity, use of pornography, and frequent masturbation associated with multiple negative emotional states) are largely absent in Mr. W's case. His sexual behavior, therefore, is most likely to represent expression of his deviant sexual interests. As such, if present, the use of sex as a coping mechanism would not be a primary dynamic factor or treatment target.

Provisional Case Formulation

As indicated in Chapter 2, treatment within the GLM and SR models begins with a case formulation that is constructed on the basis of Mr. W's dynamic risk factors (vulnerability factors) and an understanding of the manner in which these are related to his offending. The case formulation is used to construct the treatment plan for Mr. W. This is achieved by considering whether the relationship between his pursuit of human goods and his offending is direct or indirect. In addition, the goods that he seeks to achieve via offending and their implications for his personal identity, and the subsequent plan for living, should be assessed. Finally, the environment within which Mr. W is likely to be living should be taken into account and a practical action plan constructed that considers this environment.

It is evident that Mr. W's offending occurs because of consistent difficulties managing disruptive emotional states and loneliness, which in turn result from his social isolation and lack of emotional and/or competency skills. He perceives children as more accepting than adults and generally feels safer with them, indicating that his need for intimate relationships is not satisfied by adults, whom he generally avoids. This reflects a (primarily) indirect route to offending. However, there is also evidence that he seeks pleasure via sex with children and that this represents a direct relationship between his primary good of pleasure and his sexual crimes. Thus, the dynamic risk factors of intimacy deficits, social isolation, deviant sexual interests, cognitive distortions, and his tendency to feel safer with children than with adults all point to problems achieving the goods of inner peace (emotional equilibrium), relatedness, and a sense of agency (feels unsafe and threatened by adults). His personal identity appears to be directly related to his need to establish close relationships with children and his perception of the world as a dangerous place. That is, he believes that people are by nature hostile, aggressive, rejecting, and display a tendency to inflict pain and suffering on him and each other. Mr. W views himself as somewhat buffeted by life and lacks a strong locus of control. He considers himself to be vulnerable and unworthy.

Treatment should focus on providing Mr. W with the internal and external skills to achieve primary goods, with particular attention paid to the goods of social relatedness and inner peace. His tendency to relate to children primarily through sexual needs suggests a confusion of intimacy with sex and a somewhat impoverished view of close relationships. It will be crucial to strengthen Mr. W's sense of agency (autonomy good) and ability to establish connections with other adults. In addition, ways of securing sexual and other forms of pleasure should be provided.

Intervention

Based on assessment and matching of static and dynamic risk factors, Mr. W would require a high intensity sexual offender treatment program (approximately 9 to 12 months) followed by maintenance programming. This intensity level reflects the presence of multiple static risk factors and, particularly, the need in treatment to adequately assess and target, if required, deviant sexual interest/preference. The treatment portion of intervention targets for change those case specific dynamic risk factors indicated above. This process is described in detail below.

Follow-up programming (i.e., maintenance), typically of longer duration than treatment but of fewer contact hours (e.g., several hours weekly or bi-monthly), is designed to assist in the maintenance of skills acquired during treatment, rehearsal, reinforcement, the refinement of these skills and strategies, and the entrenchment and internalization of strategies to manage risk to re-offend. While supervision provides the external sources of control over behavior that may be required for a short period of time, behavior that is managed by the individual himself (i.e., internal self-regulation) is more likely than external controls to be effective in managing risk over the long-term (Yates, 2003). Mr. W will likely require higher intensity (i.e., weekly) maintenance initially following treatment as a result of his difficulties achieving primary goods and risk factors with which he presents. Once he demonstrates stable integration and management of his behavior, the frequency of contact can then be reduced.

Treatment

Generally, individuals following an avoidant-passive pathway share the treatment provider's goal of ceasing sexual offending. As such, Mr. W is likely to be amenable to treatment designed to assist him in achieving his goals, and is unlikely to be resistant to the idea of change. Thus, the first step in treatment is to establish mutually agreed-upon goals building on this pre-existing motivation to change. This process can be enhanced by identifying the particular primary goods (e.g., relatedness, mastery) most important for Mr. W, and by linking these with a set of instrumental goods that will help him to realize these goals (e.g., relationships, work, etc.). Specific strategies that will be useful at this initial stage include reinforcement of Mr. W's non-offending goal, and the use of techniques such as Socratic questioning (Beck, 1995; Beck et al., 1979; Newman, 2003) to elicit change goals from Mr. W. *What are his ultimate (higher level) goals in life? What would his ideal life look like? What has he always wanted to do? How does non-offending enhance these life goals? How can treatment help to achieve these goals? How can developing new skills help him overcome his sense of failure and worthlessness? How would life be different if he felt he had more control?* Not only does this process assist in engagement with treatment, it also functions to create a positive expectancy for treatment and commitment to treatment goals. Furthermore, the delineation of the primary goods he seeks to achieve via offending, and the fact that treatment will help him begin to achieve these goals, will also increase engagement with treatment and the sense of relevance of treatment to his life.

Despite Mr. W's likely amenability to change and to the treatment process, his engagement with treatment may be inhibited by those chronic vulnerability factors that also lead to his offending behavior. These vulnerability factors point to deficits in the internal and external conditions required to effectively achieve primary human goods. Specifically, he is likely to find it challenging to explore his offending behavior in detail as a result of the shame and sense of failure that this creates in him (lack of emotional competence skills and problems with autonomy). In addition, his difficulty establishing relationships will likely leave him struggling to develop an alliance with his treatment provider (lack of relatedness skills). What will be essential in the initial stages of treatment with Mr. W is the assistance of the therapist to help him overcome the impact of these factors on his engagement with treatment. Thus, Mr. W could be assisted to engage with treatment by using motivational strategies to explore the benefits of disclosure over continued silence and shame. As well, making transparent the requirements and parameters of the intervention, especially regarding the sharing of information requirements, may foster a sense of greater predictability about the course of treatment, thereby increasing his comfort. A review of some basic assertiveness skills may equip him to feel competent to discuss difficult topics in treatment and to interact with the treatment provider in a way that is safe. Ultimately, the initial interactions with Mr. W require that the treatment provider work toward gaining trust and instilling optimism for his ultimate ability to manage himself in a safe and healthy way.

The next phase of treatment with Mr. W consists of raising his awareness of the chronic factors which place him at risk to offend, including his difficulty establishing intimate relationships, social isolation, and sexual arousal to boys. Related to this, is helping him to grasp the fundamental goods associated with his offending – understanding what he was trying to achieve and what is important to him as a person. Although Mr. W is clearly aware that his sexual behavior is inappropriate, he lacks awareness of the relationship between these longstanding issues, primary goods, and his offending behavior. During this exercise, the treatment provider needs to be attentive to Mr. W's reactions, as the shame he feels regarding his behavior can be activated and can have a negative emotional impact on him. Required interventions, such as reinforcement of effort, normalizing his feelings, and working with him to manage these feelings, are appropriate should this occur.

In the case of Mr. W, we start to raise his awareness by having him describe his history, including all of his offending behavior, using the nine-phase self-regulation model (Figure 1). This task can be described as his opportunity to explain his life to assist the treatment provider to understand what he has experienced, as well as for him to identify those factors in his life which have left him vulnerable to engage in sexual offending. It can also help to create a link between the person he was and the person he aspires to be. The fact that his primary goods and core values remain the same (the only change required is to the manner in which he goes about securing these goods) can provide him with a sense of hope as well as generate commitment to the treatment process, since he does not need to abandon needs and goals that are important to him. During this process (to enhance his sense of confidence and to assist the therapist in developing an understanding of Mr. W's existing effective strategies) we also have him identify for us what he has done to stop or prevent himself from offending on previous occasions. Treatment builds on these existing skills and provides the opportunity to reinforce both these skills and the conviction that he possesses the ability to work toward his goals (i.e., raise self-efficacy expectations). This exercise will also provide information about his level of insight into his offending behavior, and strengthen his sense of autonomy and his ability to fashion his own future.

In addition to raising awareness, this disclosure exercise also allows both Mr. W and the treatment provider to clearly understand the links between life history, chronic vulnerability factors, dynamic risk factors, the manner in which particular life events or situations trigger the offense process, and the goods he seeks to acquire via his behavior. As indicated above, the dynamic risk factors associated with Mr. W's offending behavior include intimacy and relationship deficits, social isolation, general self-regulation, deviant sexual interests, attitudes supportive of sexual offending (possibly), the use of sex as a strategy to cope with negative emotional states, and emotional identification or comfort with children. Based on this assessment and the disclosure process, treatment targets in these areas can be refined and treatment can proceed targeting the required change in these areas. Furthermore, Mr. W is now aware of the factors that place him at risk to offend, the relationship between these factors and the specific circumstances that place him at risk, and the association between goods, vulnerability and risk factors. This exercise also assists him to appreciate the manner in which therapy can contribute to positive change.

Once Mr. W has developed an understanding of the relationships between his dynamic risk factors and his offending behavior, the second step in treatment is to identify the specific situations that initiate the offense progression. Known life events that trigger the desire to offend for Mr. W include victim access, stress with which he is unable to cope, and negative emotional states. Although additional specific circumstances are likely to be generated during the treatment process, the aim of this phase of treatment is not to identify an exhaustive list of situations that Mr. W must avoid. Rather, the objective is to identify the types of situations which, given Mr. W's vulnerability and dynamic risk factors, are likely to present a risk and for which he can develop coping strategies. The coping strategies are introduced in terms of how they can facilitate the achievement of important approach goals rather than simply removing or modifying risk factors.

In addition, Mr. W also explores his perceptions and interpretations of events surrounding the offense (prior to, during, and following the offense), and his strategy selection at the time of the offense. Mr. W is motivated by a combination of a desire for intimate contact, alleviation of social isolation or loneliness, problems with general self-regulation, and sexual urges. Mr. W must become aware of the specific internal processes that he uses that allow him, when faced with situations that place him at risk, to abandon his avoidance goal and to make the decision to progress to offending. It is crucial that he recognizes the emotional and cognitive states that allow this progression. Recall that his offending is usefully viewed as a cascade of events starting with social discomfort or dislocation (for example) and resulting in loneliness, unhappiness and ultimately sexual contact or deviant fantasies. In addition, given his possible deviant sexual preferences, he also needs to understand the contribution of sexual urges, fantasy, and interest (i.e., the primary good of pleasure).

As Mr. W does not demonstrate a high level of insight into his offending behavior at the onset of treatment, information gathering needs to be done in a non-threatening manner in order to facilitate understanding and to minimize resistance to treatment. This involves equipping him with the cognitive skills and opportunities to obtain the knowledge necessary to understand the role of offending in his life and how it is linked with his overall needs and problems (primary good of knowledge).   For these types of offenders, this phase of treatment can result in considerable frustration. Techniques that can optimize learning and decrease resistance include open-ended questioning, reflection of content and affect, allowing the offender time to generate information and links, and providing reinforcement for successful discovery. While the treatment provider should lead the offender in this process, it will be more effective to allow him to reach an understanding on his own, and to guide him in reaching this understanding, rather than to provide him with our "expert" interpretations. This can also include reiteration of the primary goods he seeks through offending, with an emphasis on reiterating these life goals and understanding how these link to his offending behavior.

Also at this stage, treatment aims to resolve the issue of attitudes supportive of sexual offending, emotional identification/congruence with children, and cognitive distortions. Specifically, the therapist can determine, on the basis of Mr. W's interpretation of offense events and precursors, whether the predominant mechanism by which he allows himself to offend is one of the cognitive distortions that justifies offending (whether he holds core beliefs or attitudes that are supportive of sexual offending against children) or whether he is more comfortable associating with children when attempting to meet intimacy and affiliation needs. Although he seeks the good of intimacy, it is still essential to uncover the precise role that cognitive distortions play in his offending behavior.

Mr. W's beliefs and attitudes shape the cognitive intervention. Modification of a belief system, whether it is that sexual activity with children is acceptable or the perception of self as affiliated with children, requires significant and long-term efforts. Treatment must, in a non-threatening manner, assist the individual to see the belief as harmful and then consistent efforts to challenge the belief must be undertaken. Clarifying the relationship between beliefs and primary goods is extremely helpful in this respect, reminding offenders that beliefs are always in the service of values and needs; they help people to extract what they think is important and worthwhile from the world. Conversely, cognitive distortions that are not reflective of core belief systems, but arise in the later phases of the offense process a result of a need to justify behavior for which the individual does not possess adequate coping strategies, require less intensive intervention.

In the case of Mr. W, cognitive distortions appear to arise from the latter process rather than reflecting a core value system that supports offending. Mr. W's goal with respect to offending is an avoidant one, and he appears to believe that sexual activity with children is wrong. However, as he moves through his progression and struggles with the conflicting goals of meeting his needs and avoiding offending, Mr. W appraises risky situations in such a way that he intensifies his personal discomfort in the areas of competence and relatedness. This triggers thoughts about having sex with children and he struggles with the dissonance between his desire to achieve intimacy, his sexual attraction to children, and his goal of not offending. His passive or avoidant reactions and thoughts of permission to engage in behaviors that are not overtly offense-related, take him closer to offending. At this point in the progression, Mr. W is likely fantasizing about prepubescent males. The failure of his system of avoidance and an increasing sense of a loss of control results in him justifying or giving himself permission to offend via a series of covert steps. Although the distortions must be challenged, in Mr. W's case, resolution of his long-standing issues (excluding deviant sexual preference; see below) and dynamic risk factors should eliminate the distortion process. The achievement of relationship goals and sexual pleasure in other ways will likely change the way he thinks about his offending. It is to be expected that deviant sexual interests will continue in the future and will lead to cognitive distortions and fantasies that he must manage. This is because there are powerful associations between sex and children. As a consequence of this, he will be at some risk to experience deviant desires in certain contexts over the long-term. At this stage, treatment also focuses on identifying the specific mechanisms by which Mr. W abandoned his avoidance goal prior to offending, creating dissonance between his beliefs and his behavior, and challenging the cognitive distortions that he used at the time of his offenses.

Prior to treatment, Mr. W indicated that he believed his behavior is wrong. As such, there exists cognitive dissonance that can be utilized in treatment, highlighting the incongruence between his beliefs and his behavior. In challenging Mr. W's cognitive distortions at the time of the offenses, the therapist can easily assist him in applying his non-offending core beliefs to the offending situation and in service of obtaining primary goods. Since there is some suggestion that he may have begun to adopt an approach goal, treatment also creates dissonance between this goal and his primary goal of avoidance, reinforcing the latter.

Thus, the focus of treatment for Mr. W with respect to cognitive distortions is two-fold. Within the context of his dynamic risk factors, the focus is on restructuring distortions, reducing minimization and justification through raising awareness of harm caused to victims, and challenging the accuracy of the distortions. This also involves assisting him to understand the manner in which cognitive distortions interfere with his life and offense goals, and the manner in which strategies to avoid engaging in the distortion process facilitates these goals. False beliefs and incorrect value judgments are likely to result in counter-productive behaviors and lower levels of well-being. Without using confrontational techniques, the treatment provider assists Mr. W to develop challenges to distortions and reinforces pro-social verbalizations. These challenges are additionally supported by regularly using positive self-talk that reinforces his goal of an offense-free lifestyle and the benefits he will ultimately achieve through that. Mr. W must monitor his appraisal about life situations and circumstances that set off the chain of events.

With respect to cognitive distortions associated with deviant sexual interest and fantasy, Mr. W must acknowledge that this will continue to pose a risk for him and will arise in future circumstances. He needs to be prepared to cope with this as well as with its associated cognitive distortions and loss of control when these occur. In addition to the cognitive restructuring described above, this represents an area of ongoing concern that Mr. W must learn to manage. Basic techniques such as thought-stopping and incompatible responses may be effective for him. For example, Mr. W may benefit from the development and reinforcement of a strategy by which he focuses on the negative consequences of offending when he finds himself sexually aroused and/or fantasizing about children. Mr. W. may also be supported to identify and explore those distortions that impede him meeting his primary good of pleasure and connectedness through the development of relationships with adult, consenting partners. As such, striving for the primary good of pleasure is supported; in this case it is the sexual interest associated with its expression that requires management.

By this stage in treatment, Mr. W will be familiar with his risk factors for offending and needs to learn a number of skills to assist himself to manage his behavior differently.

As noted above, as Mr. W's goal is to avoid offending, the primary focus of treatment is on the development of strategies to achieve this goal. His major strategies to avoid offending have been to ignore his urges and risk factors. Treatment assists him to understand how these strategies have been ineffective in meeting his goals (e.g., via Socratic questioning; Beck, 1995; Beck et al., 1979; Newman, 2003) and then would assist in the development and reinforcement of strategies to meet his needs (i.e., to secure important goods) in a non-offending manner.

Given his assessed general self-regulation deficits (specifically problem-solving), teaching him a basic problem-solving strategy would assist him to intervene in an appropriate manner as problems arise, rather than leaving him with his historical strategies of avoidance that merely results in them building up until he acts out. This strategy can be used by Mr. W at multiple points during the offense progression, including, for example, when he experiences a life event or circumstance of the type that typically triggers the offense chain for him, coping with his longer-standing difficulties (such as social isolation and relationships), extricating himself from situations in which the risk for offending may be more imminent, and as a way to manage setbacks or lapses. Such a problem-solving strategy can also assist him to cope with life events that may not be directly linked to offending behavior, such as coping with stressful situations, and to determine ways to obtain primary goods without offending in the future. This represents a general cognitive skill that facilitates more effective judgments about what is likely to be true and what is worth pursuing, and can be generalized to multiple life situations and goal achievement.

Many of Mr. W's historical harmful behaviors appear to be founded in deficits in emotional regulation and in his social interactions. As discussed above, he lacks basic skills to meet his intimacy needs. Thus, the focus of strategy development at this stage of treatment is on assisting him to acquire general social skills, and to use these skills to start developing a network of adult social relationships. Assertiveness training, including building his skills in the areas of self-expression and requesting assistance, would be useful. As he has interpersonal difficulties and describes himself as shy, he would benefit from developing cognitive strategies (such as assertiveness training) to reinforce becoming engaged with adults, in successively more interactive situations, until his intimacy needs are better met without offending, as well as coping with those situations in which these needs are not met.

At each phase in the treatment process, the therapist returns to Mr. W's lifestyle plan (i.e., plan for a better or good life), highlighting what he has achieved and what needs to happen next. The emphasis is on achieving significant personal goals rather than simply removing risk factors (although, of course, the two are linked and achieving the former tends to remove the latter). The advantage of this frequent reiteration is that individuals learn to think about their offense-related problems in a concrete and integrated manner, realizing that the most effective way to change their offending behavior is to acquire the necessary skills and resources to live a better, more satisfying life.

With respect to emotion management, especially problematic features are Mr. W's feelings of worthless, inadequacy, and loneliness/isolation, as well as the sense of guilt and shame associated with offending. The former can be alleviated, in part, by engaging in life and social activities that provide him with a sense of being worthwhile and adequate, and that serve to alleviate loneliness. In fact, we think that self-esteem is most usefully understood as reflecting individuals' core values and their subsequent evaluation about whether or not they have achieved them in a meaningful sense. What this means is that self-esteem issues should always be traced back to primary goods and the role of these in individuals' lives. In addition, Mr. W needs to examine the origin of these feelings and core beliefs in order to resolve their effects on his present state. He also needs to learn challenges to counter these feelings and to use positive self-talk in order to alleviate their effects. For example, Mr. W can elucidate those things that give him a sense of accomplishment and situations in which he experienced success, as well as positively reframe such states as loneliness. Mr. W needs to be assisted to take responsibility for offending while understanding that these behaviors are not the only thing that defines him as a person. His readiness to create social relationships will be impacted upon by his shame. That is, he is likely to consider himself to be defective as a person, and consequently believe that other people will want to avoid social contact with him. He must be supported to "make good". The GLM model can be used to help him understand this process. In this way, it acts as a map for being different and can increase commitment and optimism about change and the future.

To that end, Mr. W should be supported to work toward achieving a greater sense of satisfaction with his life. His sense of satisfaction may increase by expanding his leisure and other activities that help him develop better balance, decrease isolation, and increase social activity. His commitment to an offense-free lifestyle will be positively influenced by this process, as he can use gains to reinforce his commitment.

Mr. W will also need to develop strategies to manage deviant sexual arousal and fantasy, based on the outcome of assessment in this area. Arousal reconditioning techniques that extinguish deviant arousal and increase appropriate arousal (Marshall et al., 1999; Yates et al., 2000) are procedures that may be used to assist him to manage these urges, as well as the cognitive techniques described previously. Mr. W. will continue to experience a need for pleasure and sexual release, so he must be prepared to develop cognitive strategies to support him to explore healthy outlets for his sexual expression. Although one goal is to eliminate deviant arousal to boys, it is essential that reconditioning to increase age-appropriate arousal also be conducted, in order that he can meet his sexual needs in the future without offending. Should Mr. W retain his preference for prepubescent boys, he would need to be aware that this will be a lifelong challenge for him to manage. He will need to recognize that fantasies and thoughts about offending represent a lapse that will take him one step closer to offending. He must use his skills to ensure that he does not engage in masturbatory fantasies about boys, to attempt to broaden his interests for a consenting partner, and to find alternative ways to experience both sexual and other forms of pleasure.

While learning these new skills, it is essential that Mr. W be guided to practice his skills in a manner that results in success experiences, which will reinforce these new strategies, increasing his self-efficacy and outcome expectations. This will guard against the loss of control that occurs when he is faced with situations that place him at risk. In addition, treatment must uncover and reinforce Mr. W's existing skills, focusing on those situations in which he managed emotions effectively, countered cognitive distortions appropriately, and those instances in which he prevented himself in the past from offending and was able to achieve goals without offending. These strategies represent an existing skill set that is likely to be at least already partially entrenched which can be used in future to avoid re-offending.

The final stage in treatment with Mr. W is to highlight the need for him to self-monitor on a regular basis to ensure that he is coping effectively with risk situations, is implementing effective strategies to prevent offending, and is experiencing success in obtaining primary goods. The identification of the internal and external cues/triggers that lead to his loss of control is important to that process. Of course, from a GLM perspective, this means ensuring that he is implementing his lifestyle plan in a manner that is sensitive to local circumstances and responsive to threats or disruptions.

One of Mr. W's significant triggers is victim access. As such, he must identify as many situations as possible in which he would have access to potential victims. Avoidance of these circumstances is the best intervention until he has internalized his skills. He needs to ensure that his needs for social contact are factored into his daily routines, and that he has ample opportunities to realize the goods of relatedness in ways that are personally satisfying and socially acceptable.

However, as Mr. W is likely not able to avoid all places where prepubescent boys frequent, he should also explicitly plan for these situations. He also needs to be prepared to use his assertiveness skills to seek assistance to facilitate extricating himself from such situations. For example, he might find himself alone on a bus with a boy. Should such a situation occur, Mr. W needs to appraise the situation to see if there are safe ways to handle it until he can remove himself. For example, he can move as far as possible away from the boy, perhaps sit near the driver, and then use positive self-talk to maintain his commitment by recalling his goal to not hurt victims, the gains he has made, and the consequences to breaching his goals. He also needs to be prepared to remove himself from such a situation should his strategies prove ineffective, after which he must revisit his responses with his treatment or maintenance therapist and/or supervisor in order to deconstruct the situation and revisit his self-regulation plan and to prepare to respond more effectively in future situations. He may need to develop other strategies that will have a higher likelihood of being effective. Given his past tendency to lose control and to give up, Mr. W must be assisted to view this situation as a learning experience on which he can build in order to respond more effectively in the future.

In situations in which Mr. W anticipates that he might have access to a potential victim, he can consider such short-term strategies as attending with a support person, ensuring that he monitors his appraisal of any boys he encounters, and challenging any deviant thoughts or fantasies he may experience. Furthermore, he should cognitively prepare for such situations in advance, focusing on the negative consequences of any lapse in thinking or behavior. In these situations, he can also use positive and reinforcing self-talk to enable him to remain focused on his goals. When he successfully manages such situations, a review of his management plan and the use of positive reinforcement for successful coping will help him develop a greater sense of confidence and competence to manage his life. Ultimately, the goal of treatment and maintenance is to reduce the need to manage such situations via both effective self-regulation (i.e., risk management) and the attainment of primary goods via the establishment of appropriate relationships that meet his needs (e.g., intimacy, pleasure).

As stated throughout this manual, assisting Mr. W to develop short-term and long-term goals for a more satisfying life is an important component in treatment. Social connectedness has already featured prominently. It should also span multiple domains, including such things as employment/education and leisure. Treatment should identify and assist Mr. W in those areas not directly associated with sexual offending but that will increase his achievement of higher-order life goals, such as acquiring employment, continuing education, engaging in spiritual or cultural activities, or becoming involved in satisfying leisure or recreational activities. For Mr. W, the relationship between primary human goods and his offending behavior appears to be mainly indirect. That is, as a consequence of loneliness, frustration, and a sense of unworthiness, he becomes despondent and is then more likely to act in a sexually aggressive manner. His lack of a sense of agency (autonomy good) is a marked feature of his presentation, alongside problems in establishing relationships with adults. Children appear to offer him emotional support and a sense of intimacy.

Maintenance and Supervision

When in a community setting (either during treatment or following treatment while incarcerated), Mr. W would also participate in supervision (i.e., via parole or probation services) designed to monitor his risk to re-offend and his community functioning. This supervision would assist in ensuring that his plan for living a better life was running smoothly and that routes to re-offending were not being reopened. Assessment and treatment reports, including self-regulation plans, are a valuable source of information for identifying factors that need to be monitored to manage the case. In this case, supervision would entail restricting and monitoring Mr. W's access to prepubescent boys, supporting him in establishing age-appropriate social relationships, and monitoring social isolation, coping with loneliness, and coping with feelings of low self-worth. As indicated above, there are a number of static and dynamic risk factors that are not present in Mr. W's case. Specifically, he has not committed any non-contact sexual offenses and has not engaged in non-sexual violent behavior or other criminal behavior. As such, these are unlikely to represent treatment or supervision issues for Mr. W.

Mr. W would benefit from participation in maintenance programming after he completes treatment. Supervision should be augmented by regular case conferences between the parole/probation officer and the treatment provider as this provides multi-source reports on Mr. W's management of his risk factors and his progress toward achieving his goals. Facilitating and reinforcing Mr. W's ability to cope with his deviant interest/preference is more likely to be within the domain of the treatment provider, but is also pertinent information for the supervisor.

Adjunctive intervention, such as Circles of Support (Wilson & Prinzo, 2001; Wilson et al., 2003), may also provide Mr. W with additional pro-social community support that can assist in the management of risk to re-offend. In addition, Mr. W's parents are supportive of him and have encouraged him to participate in treatment. As such, they are pro-social, positive resources upon which Mr. W can rely in the community. Their support for treatment suggests that they are unlikely to collude with Mr. W should he engage in cognitive distortions surrounding his offenses, and could additionally be relied upon to assist him in the implementation of his self-regulation and good life plans, to monitor any changes in his risk, and to work closely with the community supervision officer, including reporting any difficulties Mr. W may experience.

Community intervention could also entail assisting him to find employment (if he has not retained his current employment), ensuring that this work remains meaningful for him, and making sure the work environment is conducive to risk management.

Balancing community safety, for example via disclosure, without setting up the offender for failure, requires careful evaluation. Disclosure of offending and risk factors to employers, and to newly developed networks of acquaintances and friends must be done cautiously. Mr. W would need to be supported to evaluate the potential risks of each circumstance and, when the decision for disclosure is taken, manage this in a way that increases the probability of a positive outcome. For example, Mr. W's work supervisor could be apprised of his offenses, in order to assist in monitoring, as well as to assist Mr. W to avoid work social functions at which the children of other employees would be present (e.g., company holiday parties). As one of his treatment tasks is developing a social network, he will need to be aware that it is likely he will need to disclose his offense history and risk factors to certain people under certain circumstances. He will need to be able to cope with personal rejection, negative emotional states, and the threat to goal attainment that this rejection entails.

Chapter 6: Treatment Implications for Offenders Following an Avoidant-active Pathway

Case Example Synopsis

Mr. N was convicted of indecently touching his biological daughter when she was ten years old. At that time, Mr. N had been working for an organization in Africa identifying and working with girls who had been abused via prostitution. He lived with his wife and children in a physically open environment in which family members were frequently partially clothed as a result of the hot climate. Mr. N became sexually aroused to his daughter in this situation. Although he believed she was behaving seductively, he realized his arousal was inappropriate and attempted to avoid high risk contact with her. In some instances, he was successful in achieving this goal. In other situations, however, he became aroused and acted out sexually, via fondling her and approaching sexual intercourse. Mr. N initially denied sexual intent. However, he later fully admitted his offenses, served a prison term, and successfully completed treatment. Although Mr. N has no prior sexual offenses, he had previously experienced sexual arousal to an eleven-year-old girl whom he was babysitting. He told his wife about this immediately and ensured that he did not baby-sit alone following this incident. Children's services are involved with Mr. N and his family in order to effect gradual reunification.

Pathway Allocated: Avoidant-active

Within the self-regulation model of offending, the avoidant-active pathway is characterized as a mis-regulation pathway, in which the individual desires to avoid sexual offending (an inhibitory goal) and attempts to refrain from offending via the active implementation of strategies. However, these strategies are ineffective and, in some cases, may serve to increase risk via reinforcement of the desire to offend and of offending behavior. When these individuals are faced with situations that trigger the desire to offend, they expect that their self-regulation strategies will be effective in managing the situation. They are likely to experience negative affective states associated with offending behavior and failure to achieve their non-offending goal.

Mr. N is allocated to the avoidant-active pathway to offending due to his desire to avoid offending and his attempts to refrain from offending. Examples of these attempts include avoiding his daughter on certain occasions and avoiding situations in which he would be alone with the eleven-year-old girl (following his experience of sexual arousal while babysitting on the earlier occasion). Although he prevented himself from offending against his daughter on some occasions, he failed on others, and also remained in a situation that placed him at risk. Specifically, the family remained in Africa and he continued to work with sexually explicit materials in a sexually-charged environment. He finally removed himself and his family from this environment, returning to the UK, where he served his prison term. Similarly, during the earlier incident when he became sexually aroused while babysitting, Mr. N took steps to ensure this did not recur, by ensuring that he did not baby-sit again. As such, Mr. N demonstrated strategies to avoid offending on numerous occasions, although he appears to have relied predominantly on an avoidance strategy.

Identified Risk Factors

Prior to treatment, risk factors are identified to evaluate Mr. N's risk for sexual re-offending based on static and dynamic factors. This assessment provides information necessary for program matching, developing treatment targets, and supervision.

Static Risk Factors. Actuarial risk assessment measures risk to re-offend relative to other sexual offenders, using static factors empirically demonstrated to be predictive of recidivism. Using actuarial assessment of static risk (Static-99; Hanson & Thornton, 1999), with a score of 0, Mr. N's risk factors as assessed using this scale place him at a low risk to re-offend relative to other sexual offenders. Normative data for offenders falling into this category demonstrate a probability of sexual recidivism of 5%, 11%, and 13% over 5, 10, and 15 years, respectively.

Mr. N is unlikely to present a risk for violent or general criminal behavior. He has no history of nonsexual violence or other criminality, nor is there evidence of attitudes supportive of crime, or identification or association with pro-criminal others. Mr. N presents as generally pro-social in areas other than his sexual offending behavior. For example, he has stable employment and positive community support from his family.

Dynamic Risk Factors/Treatment Targets. Dynamic risk factors are those factors empirically demonstrated to be predictive of sexual recidivism that can be changed through intervention. The following treatment targets for Mr. N were based on case-specific factors as assessed against these dynamic risk factors, such as those described within the Stable 2000 (Hanson & Harris, 2004).

- Intimacy/relationship deficits
- Cognitive distortions
- Deviant sexual arousal/interest (provisional)

Mr. N reported that, following the birth of their first child (the daughter against whom he later offended) he felt jealous of his wife's attention and affection toward the baby. He avoided both his wife and his daughter. Later, while in Africa, the sexual relationship with his wife diminished and Mr. N felt excluded and resentful of the time Mrs. N spent with the children. Mrs. N also experienced some health problems at that time, which likely contributed to the diminishment of their sexual relationship and to Mr. N's feelings of resentment. Mr. N first reported sexual arousal to his daughter at this time, and began to engage in sexual fantasies about her.

Although he believes that his sexual arousal is inappropriate, during both the babysitting incident and prior to offending against his daughter, Mr. N engaged in cognitive distortions in which he rationalized his behavior as being provoked by the girls. Specifically, he indicated that he believed that both the girl whom he babysat and his daughter were flirting with him or "coming onto him". During the time he worked in Africa, such distortions were reinforced by men who exploited young girls for prostitution, whom he said were "persuasive", and by the girls themselves, who indicated that, by comparison to their previous life circumstances, their abusive situations in prostitution were an improvement. These experiences reinforced Mr. N's cognitive distortions. In addition, his work in a sexually-charged environment and his exposure to pornography also served to reinforce these distortions.

Despite these distortions, however, Mr. N consistently believed that his sexual arousal was wrong, and he felt guilty when thinking sexually about his daughter and the other girl, and when acting out or fantasizing. This suggests that the cognitive distortions in which Mr. N engaged were specifically related to his offense progression, and are not reflective of attitudes or core beliefs that support sexual offending.

There is some suggestion that Mr. N may present with deviant sexual arousal or interest, a feature that requires further assessment. Had his sexual arousal been limited to the occasions on which he offended against his daughter, Mr. N would likely be considered a "typical" incest offender, who came to regard his daughter in an adult role as a result of a distant relationship with his wife. However, Mr. N did not report his sexual arousal to his daughter as having a basis in her being a "substitute" or surrogate for his wife in either a sexual or intimate context. That is, Mr. N does not report that he viewed his daughter as an adult partner in the absence of having his needs met by his wife. In addition, Mr. N had also experienced sexual arousal to the eleven-year-old girl in the babysitting incident, which is not consistent with a classic incest profile. Finally, although he reported that he felt "sad", Mr. N also reported that he became aroused when viewing pornography as part of his job in Africa.

What is unknown in each of these incidents, however, is the object of Mr. N's sexual interest that triggered sexual arousal. Specifically, if each of the girls toward whom he became aroused evidenced secondary sexual characteristics (e.g., breasts, pubic hair, etc.), Mr. N may not have demonstrated deviant interests in prepubescent females. Although this requires confirmation through additional assessment, it is likely (given the girls' ages) that they lacked such characteristics and that Mr. N has some sexual interest in prepubescent or pubescent girls. As such, it is likely that Mr. N requires intervention in this area. Although there may be some interest, there is minimal evidence to suggest a primary deviant sexual preference. Mr. N prefers his adult sexual relationship with his wife. Again, this should be confirmed through additional assessment throughout treatment.

Finally, Mr. N requires some intervention to cope with negative emotional states. During his offense progression, he was unable to cope with lack of attention from his wife on several occasions, and this was integral to his offending behavior.

Provisional Case Formulation

As indicated in Chapter 2, treatment within the GLM and SR models begins with a case formulation that is constructed on the basis of Mr. N's dynamic risk factors (vulnerability factors) and an understanding of the manner in which these are related to his offending. This formulation is then used to construct the treatment plan for Mr. N. This is achieved by considering whether the relationship between his pursuit of human goods and his offending is direct or indirect. In addition, Mr. N's overarching goods should be noted, as well as their implication for his personal identity and subsequent plan for living. Finally, the environment in which Mr. N is likely to be living should be taken into account and a practical action plan constructed.

It appears that Mr. N was feeling sexually and personally rejected by his wife around the time of his offense, indicating problems in achieving the good of relatedness as well as a sense of being loved and cared for. He struggled to express this in an effective way or to understand that his wife's apparent withdrawal was triggered by her ill health and increased responsibilities. This indicates some problems with agency and autonomy, and the possibility that he feels like he is an individual who is able to "give" to others and yet feels at times he does not receive the recognition he merits. The fact that he worked for a social service agency dealing with vulnerable children points to the good of community and is a real strength. He presents as a man who is caring toward others and sensitive to the damage he has inflicted on both his wife and his daughter. There is also some suggestion that Mr. N instrumentally seeks sexual pleasure through deviant fantasies and behavior involving young girls. It seems that a combination of perceived rejection, lack of intimacy, ineffective emotional coping, the pressure of helping others, and a sense that his own needs were not being met, in an environment where the sexual boundaries between adults and children were loosened, culminated in his sexual abuse of his daughter. Thus, the route to his offending appears to be primarily indirect.

Treatment should seek to capitalize on his sense of integrity and determination to do the best for others. Mr. N's personal identity revolves around his perception of himself as a just and caring man who is committed to the rights and needs of others (the good of community). Thus, his strong social conscience and desire to help others ought to be a major focus, although tempered by the need for Mr. N to realize that it is imperative that he expresses his needs to help others in appropriate ways. This difficulty points to some subtle problems in autonomy and a tendency to subjugate his needs to others on occasions. Treatment should, therefore, look for opportunities to help Mr. N express his needs and yet not expect that this means that others will necessarily always be able to meet them. Also, Mr. N should be encouraged to meet his needs on his own, without reliance on others.

Intervention

Based on assessment and matching of static and dynamic risk factors, Mr. N requires minimal intervention for both treatment and supervision. He would benefit from a low intensity sexual offender treatment program (approximately 3 to 6 months), followed by minimal follow-up maintenance programming. This intensity level reflects Mr. N's low risk to re-offend relative to other sexual offenders, and the minimal dynamic risk factors requiring intervention. Similarly, Mr. N's probation/parole supervision needs are routine and minimal.

Treatment

Generally, individuals following an avoidant-active pathway share the treatment provider's goal of ceasing sexual offending. In Mr. N's case, it is clear that he is amenable to treatment designed to assist him in achieving his goals and refraining from re-offending, and that he is unlikely to be resistant to the idea of change. He clearly regards his offending behavior as wrong, and on multiple occasions has demonstrated the capacity to implement effective intervention strategies. Mr. N is likely to welcome intervention to assist him to develop additional skills to effectively manage those situations in which his strategies have not proven effective. A primary aim of therapy will be to help Mr. N detect the instrumental goods sought via his offending and the ways in which these are associated with the primary goods of autonomy, relatedness, community, and inner peace (emotional competence).

There is, however, one area of intervention to which Mr. N could possibly demonstrate some resistance. Specifically, as described above, there is indication that he may have some deviant sexual interests, and this area has not heretofore been addressed with him. Given Mr. N's sexual values, core beliefs that sexual offending is wrong, his social standing in his community, the importance of the good of community in his life, the importance of his family, his experience of shame related to his offending behavior, and his desire and work to help others who are abused, there is a high probability that he will respond to initial intervention in this area with shame, which may cause him to become defensive and to resist treatment in this area. As such, any intervention in this area, including any awareness-raising interventions, should not be attempted until Mr. N has been in treatment for a period of time, has developed a positive working alliance with the treatment provider, and has a sense of safety in treatment. When the issue of his possible deviant sexual interests is addressed, it would be useful if the therapist presented it in the context of his strong sense of community (and associated values such as fairness, rights of others, and justice) and his tendency at times to relegate his own needs for sex and intimacy to a secondary position. This strategy will capitalize on Mr. N's strengths while at the same time pointing out that denial of his needs for intimacy (and sex) can result in a cascading sequence of events leading (indirectly) to sexual offending. Recall that a critical component of Mr. N's personal identity resides in his commitment to the good of the community and the rights of other people. Emphasizing such values will help to motivate him to reflect on the factors associated with his sexual offending and also provide a template for a new way of living – one that is attuned to these core values (i.e., a good lives plan) but also decreases his risk of committing further offenses (i.e., risk management).

Much of treatment with Mr. N will involve uncovering the dynamics of his offending behavior against his daughter along the lines sketched out above. Mr. N does not fit an obvious sexual offender profile. Specifically, he is obviously not pedophilic, nor does he fit the profile of the "classic" incest offender in that, given the available information, he does not appear to have placed his daughter in the role of a surrogate partner for his wife. Although he demonstrates some mild sexual interest in prepubescent or pubescent girls, he does not evidence sexual deviance and prefers adult heterosexual sexual relationships. With respect to incest, he does not evidence dynamics such as feelings of sexual entitlement or anger at his wife as a result of his needs being unmet, although he did report some resentment toward her. Rather, he sometimes seems to dismiss his own needs as unimportant and then struggles to deal with the resulting feelings of rejection, loneliness, deprivation, and sexual frustration. Alternatively, he may place too great a responsibility on others to meet his needs (e.g., his wife), feeling rejected or resentful when this does not occur. Given these various possibilities, much of the treatment interventions described below are designed to assist both the therapist and Mr. N in understanding why he came to offend.

The first step in treatment is to establish mutually agreed-upon goals that build on Mr. N's motivation to avoid offending and his existing strategies, so he can better manage his behavior should similar situations arise in the future. Specific intervention techniques that will be useful at this initial stage include reinforcement of Mr. N's non-offending goal and his existing effective strategies. Specifically, Mr. N should understand that his strategy of removing himself from situations that place him at risk is effective and should be maintained. Later in treatment (see below), Mr. N can be guided to analyze those situations in which his strategies were not effective, with the aim of understanding why these were ineffective, and he can then be encouraged to generate new strategies (particularly those that are not predominantly avoidance-based) which have a higher likelihood of being successful. Although not a typically recommended or effective intervention strategy with most offenders, Mr. N is likely to be amenable to advice and suggestions from the treatment provider with respect to these new strategies, given his strong motivation to refrain from offending and his advanced stage of change. In addition, once he begins to grasp that his good lives plan lacks sufficient scope and that he has tended to ignore important primary goods such as pleasure, play, relatedness (intimacy), and so on, he can start to focus on achieving the capabilities and resources to lead a more balanced lifestyle. In Mr. N's case, his offending is indirectly triggered by his failure to secure important human goods, and most significantly, a sense of estrangement from others.

The next phase of treatment with Mr. N consists of raising his awareness of the chronic factors that place him at risk to offend. Specifically, this includes the difficulties he experienced in his relationship with his wife during situations in which he was unable to cope with her attention and affection being directed more toward the family and less toward him. He needs to understand the need for this attention, his inability to cope with its absence or diminution, the negative emotions he experiences in such situations, and the manner in which this inhibits goal achievement, with the goal of ultimately developing strategies to cope with each of these factors. The links between the absence of attention, etc., should also be discussed alongside the recognition that he tends to devalue his own needs in the interests of the community and others. Although Mr. N is clearly aware that his sexual offending behavior was inappropriate, he lacks awareness of the relationship between these fundamental issues (relating to scope, capacity, and conflict problems in his good lives plan) and his offending behavior. Helping Mr. N to reflect systematically on the relationship between his (human) needs, lifestyle, and subsequent offending will strengthen his ability to function autonomously in the future. As indicated above, this type of intervention should be undertaken with no or minimal reference to deviant sexual interest at this early stage in treatment.

We start to raise Mr. N's awareness by having him describe the circumstances surrounding the sexual offense he committed against his daughter, using the nine-phase self-regulation model (Figure 1). This task can be described as his opportunity to explain the situation in order to assist the treatment provider to understand what he has experienced, as well as for him to identify those factors which left him vulnerable to offending during the time he lived in Africa. It can also be pointed out that it will help the therapist to grasp what Mr. N values in life and what he was directly or indirectly seeking via sexual offending. During this exercise, Mr. N needs to be encouraged to explore the manner in which his work at that time placed him at risk and reinforced his offense progression. In addition, Mr. N needs to describe both the occasions on which he acted out sexually against his daughter and those on which he was able to control his arousal and to refrain from offending against her. In analyzing the differences between these occasions, Mr. N will be assisted to identify and differentiate between those strategies that were effective and those that were not. This will also allow him to begin to examine his vulnerability factors, including problems in his intimate relationship with his wife, his tendency to elevate community concerns above his own, his inability to cope with negative affect related to these problems, and his sexual arousal to his daughter. During this exercise, reinforcement of Mr. N's desire to avoid offending, his existing effective strategies, and his pro-social life objectives, will assist in reinforcing his non-offending goals, and will enhance his sense of confidence and self-efficacy with respect to avoiding offending in future. This exercise will provide the treatment provider with information about Mr. N's level of insight into his offending behavior. In addition to understanding the offense progression, this disclosure exercise also allows both Mr. N and the treatment provider to understand clearly the links between his chronic vulnerability factors, and the manner in which these triggered the offense process. Significantly, Mr. N will acquire an understanding of what particular goods are most clearly associated with his sexual offending. The availability of this information is likely to provide a set of approach goals that can be used to construct and refine a subsequent treatment plan and to motivate him to acquire adaptive ways of achieving the outcomes he values most. Based on this understanding, treatment targets in these areas can be refined, and treatment can proceed targeting the required change in these areas.

The next stage in treatment with Mr. N involves examination of his attitudes and beliefs toward sexual offending, and examination of the cognitive distortions he used to allow himself to proceed in the offense progression and to take the decision to offend. As indicated above, Mr. N's cognitive distortions are not seen to be reflective of a core belief system or attitudes that support sexual offending. Rather, he engaged in cognitive distortions in the latter phases of the offense progression as a result of a need to reduce dissonance and to justify behavior which he clearly believed was inappropriate but which he could not control as a result of ineffective self-regulation strategies. These cognitive distortions functioned to protect Mr. N's self-esteem and to maintain his view that he was a caring individual who typically put the need and interests of others ahead of his own. It is necessary for him to grasp that, while he is typically concerned with helping others, in the context of his offending it was the failure to meet certain needs of his own that resulted in the sexual abuse of his daughter. The sexual abuse of his daughter demonstrated a *lack of concern* for her welfare and the indulgence of his own desires at the expense of her real interests. Paradoxically, it was because he held such values that he construed his offending in a manifestly distorted and self-serving manner; in order to deflect self-criticism. Because of the function of cognitive distortions and the fact that these do not represent underlying attitudes that support sexual aggression, required intervention in this area with Mr. N is less intensive than would be required with an individual who possesses core beliefs that sexual offending is acceptable.

When faced with the situation in which he experienced sexual attraction or interest toward his daughter, Mr. N interpreted innocuous behavior, such as giggling, as sexual interest on her part. This is in part due to the powerful needs he experienced for closeness and pleasure, and his reluctance (or inability) to directly communicate his needs to others and/or to cope with the temporary loss of this pleasure as a result of transitory circumstances affecting his relationship with his wife. Again, it is also important to stress the relationship between this failure and Mr. N's strong orientation to others and the community. This tactic will make it easier for him to make the appropriate links and will also attenuate any tendency to engage in fruitless self-condemnation. The extent to which his daughter's innocuous behavior influenced Mr. N's decision to proceed to offending is, at this stage, unknown. Similarly, the extent to which he interpreted his daughter's partial nudity (as a result of the hot African climate) as sexually provocative is also unclear. As such, the goal of treatment at this stage is two-fold. First, Mr. N needs to analyze his interpretations and cognitive responses to these situations in detail. Second, he needs to examine the reasons why he interpreted his daughter's behavior as provocative. It is likely that he interpreted multiple behaviors and situations as sexually provocative, and that he engaged in cognitive distortions as a mechanism to justify acting out sexually when he found he was unable to control his sexual arousal and to meet his needs. The fact that he has a strong sense of the rights and interests of others would make it difficult for Mr. N sexually offend without engaging in these kinds of cognitive gymnastics. Thus, intervention in this area needs to assist Mr. N to uncover and to understand these dynamics and issues. The extent to which his work in Africa and his exposure to explicit and abusive sexuality contributed to his cognitive distortions and manner of thinking with respect to his daughter also requires examination along the lines described above.

The above goals can be achieved via an analysis of his progression to offending, in a step-by-step fashion, using a process by which Mr. N elaborates, in detail and with the assistance of the therapist via Socratic questioning (Beck, 1995; Beck et al., 1979; Newman, 2003), exactly what occurred prior to, during, and following offending and on all occasions on which he experienced inappropriate sexual arousal. *What was he thinking at each moment in time during the offense progression, beginning when he first noticed his daughter in a sexual way? What did she do that he interpreted as sexually provocative? At what point did he realize he was experiencing sexual arousal? Did he try to manage this arousal? If, so, how, and why did this fail? Given that he believes his behavior is wrong, how did he overcome this belief and permit himself to offend? What was he hoping to experience? What was he seeking to achieve via offending (i.e., what was his goal)?*

In terms of the larger context, Mr. N will examine the nature of his relationship with his wife at the time of his offenses, including his feelings and needs at that time. The aim is to understand why he sought to meet his needs with his daughter rather than with his wife, as well as the reasons for which he was unable to cope with the loss of intimacy. *In what areas of his relationship was he feeling deprived? Was he seeking sexual gratification or to meet his intimacy needs, or both? What was the nature of his relationship with his wife at that time? Was this a temporary situation or a chronic problem in their relationship? How important does he regard his own needs compared to those of others? How much time does he spend having fun versus working or helping other people? What important activities were missing from his life at the time? How was he not adequately meeting his need to contribute to the good of community?* The aim is also to confirm that Mr. N had not come to regard his daughter as a surrogate partner (i.e., to evaluate his status as an incest offender). *How much time was Mr. N spending with his daughter? What did they do during the time they spent together? Were they doing things together that Mr. N would normally have done with his wife, who, due to illness and family responsibilities, was unavailable? Had there been a change in the amount and quality of time that Mr. N and his daughter spent together?*

In addition, as noted above, Mr. N was working in a highly sexually charged environment at the time of his offenses. As part of the above-indicated analysis of his offense progression, the influence of this environment is examined in addition to Mr. N's own cognitive processes and behavior. *What was the influence of the environment in which he worked at that time? What did he think about what the men who abused the girls in Africa had said, and why did he regard them as "persuasive"? What was so persuasive about their arguments? Did he use these ideas to justify his sexual arousal and his sexual offending behavior against his daughter?*

Mr. N's social relationships during the time he lived in Africa are also pertinent to the analysis of his offense progression. *Did he have relationships other than work and family during this time? Did he and Mrs. N have an active social life, or was their time limited to work and family? Was he experiencing social isolation, or a decline in social relationships, at the time?* The aim of this line of questioning is to determine whether there was a change in Mr. N's social network and activity that may have led him to feel socially and emotionally isolated and/or a chronic condition which resulted in his needs remaining unmet, and that may have resulted in him turning to his daughter to meet his needs.

During this analysis, Mr. N should be able to clearly identify the cognitive distortions in which he engaged in both situations in which he attended to his daughter in a sexual way and those in which he acted out. What is essential to understand in Mr. N's case is how it is possible, given that he is pro-social in all other aspects of his life, his high level of skill, his belief that his offending behavior is wrong, and his desire to help others who are harmed and to contribute to the overall health of his community, that he eventually came to offend. In our view, it is reasonably clear. However, it is crucial that Mr. N come to his own realization concerning the relationship between his lifestyle and sexual offending. He should be able to identify and generate the specific cognitive mechanisms by which he was able to overcome his core belief systems in the specific situations in which he offended against his daughter. In addition, it would be helpful for him to grasp the relationship between these cognitive processes and his struggle to secure important goods in his life. Like most people, Mr. N needs to feel loved and close to other people, and to feel they value him for who he is. If this is absent, then it is only to be expected he will look for it elsewhere. If the alternatives involve wrongful actions, then it is likely Mr. N will attempt to avoid or escape from the resulting self-condemnation through the use of cognitive distortions. If he has difficulty identifying arousal and cognitive distortions, the treatment provider may facilitate this process by having Mr. N compare the situations in which he offended to those when he did not, and analyze the differences between these two. This technique may also assist the therapist should Mr. N demonstrate any resistance during this exercise that may result from his sense of embarrassment and/or shame at his actions, which might inhibit disclosure. In addition, this will allow Mr. N to discuss, and to be reinforced for, the times during which he coped effectively and successfully.

It is expected that such a disclosure exercise will be very difficult for Mr. N, possibly causing him considerable shame, which may result in some resistance. This resistance is most likely to be in the form of a superficial analysis of his behavior, as the details will be shame-inducing, and may also manifest itself as defensiveness on Mr. N's part. It is essential that the therapist create a safe environment for disclosure as well as reinforcing Mr. N's efforts, in order to facilitate additional disclosure and analysis using the tactic outlined above (e.g., utilizing his community orientation, tendency to deny his own desires, etc.). At this phase in treatment, the aim is to raise Mr. N's awareness of the factors that led to his offending behavior. Until he is able to identify these factors and to cope with the negative emotional reactions this may generate, the therapist should not begin challenging his cognitive distortions, and should ensure that s/he does not respond in a judgmental manner to Mr. N's disclosures. Doing so at this time could cause Mr. N to withdraw from the treatment process.

One of the attractive features of the GLM is that it allows therapist to focus on deficits and dynamic risk factors, while also addressing areas of strength. Focusing on what Mr. N was seeking and wanting from his life and how his failure to achieve these indirectly or directly resulted in his offending, can reduce shame. It can achieve this by reminding offenders that they are human beings who need and look for the same kinds of goods all people do. It can also clarify to them exactly what their global value commitments are, what kind of life they would like to have, and person they want to be.

By the end of this disclosure exercise, both the therapist and Mr. N should have a clearer understanding of the dynamics of his offending behavior, and the questions surrounding his reasons for offending, indicated above, should be resolved. For example, if Mr. N has disclosed sexual entitlement sentiments and/or anger at his wife that suggest he placed his daughter in a surrogate partner role, we would be able to conclude that Mr. N likely fits the profile of the classic incest offender. Conversely, (as is most likely) we could learn that Mr. N's behavior resulted almost entirely from his social and work situation, such as social isolation and exposure to an abusive environment through his work.

Given that, at this stage in treatment, the dynamics of Mr. N's offending are known, the next step in treatment is to explore the babysitting incident, in which Mr. N experienced sexual arousal to an eleven-year-old girl, in order to determine whether this incident is consistent with his offending behavior against his daughter or whether there exist other factors that need to be considered and addressed in treatment (e.g., deviant sexual interest). This incident is explored similarly to his offending against his daughter. Specifically, the disclosure process described above is used to confirm offense dynamics and treatment targets. This also assists Mr. N in uncovering behavioral and cognitive patterns and similarities between these incidents. Additionally, it can clarify and/or confirm what approach goals (goods) Mr. N was seeking and how these relate to his offending. Furthermore, this information can be used to fine-tune the treatment plan or to simply reiterate to Mr. N that his sexually abusive actions emerged from a problematic lifestyle and dysfunctional ways of securing important goals.

The next step in treatment is to confirm or eliminate the existence of deviant sexual interest on the part of Mr. N. This begins with an examination of Mr. N's sexual history and attitudes. Based on available information, it appears that Mr. N is quite conservative in his sexual values and may have a tendency to repress his sexuality. For example, he indicated that he felt guilty when he engaged in sexual activity in college prior to his marriage to his wife, and that he disapproves of sexual activity outside marriage. He also has some conservative gender role attitudes that developed when he was young which, in combination with his sexual conservativism, may make it hard for him to develop deep intimacy within romantic relationships. Little information is available on the nature of his sexual relationship with his wife, and their satisfaction with this aspect of their relationship, as well their relationship as a whole. As such, Mr. N is unlikely to seek sexual gratification outside his sexual relationship with his wife, including via the use of pornography or fantasy and/or masturbation in those situations when the frequency of their sexual relations had diminished as a result of extraneous circumstances. Thus, the working hypothesis at this stage of treatment is that, as a result of his core values regarding sexuality and romantic relationships, Mr. N had no other sexual outlet that did not make him feel bad or guilty during the two known periods when his sexual relationship with his wife worsened. He also tended to regard his own desires and needs as somewhat unimportant and, thus, failed to communicate his sense of frustration and loneliness when feeling rejected. These factors, in combination with the very specific circumstances in Africa at the time of his offending, at least partially contributed to his offending behavior.

Information obtained from the above-indicated sexual history analysis will reveal other instances of deviant arousal or interest, and resolve the question of the object of Mr. N's sexual arousal as well as the content of his sexual fantasies. Specifically, it will be known whether his daughter and the eleven-year-old girl in the babysitting incident had begun to develop sexually and to show secondary sex characteristics. It will also be known whether Mr. N's sexual fantasies involve solely adults and whether his sexual preference is for adults (as is likely in this case). If this is the case, we can conclude that Mr. N's arousal was not deviant, particularly if it is also evident that it was linked solely to those periods during which sexual activity and intimacy with his wife had diminished.

Regardless of the outcome of the above-indicated assessment, once this is done, the treatment provider assists Mr. N in understanding that he has demonstrated a pattern of inappropriate sexual responding in more than one situation. It is essential to future risk management that Mr. N understands that his offensive behavior toward his daughter was not an isolated incident, but that he has demonstrated a pattern of inappropriate sexual arousal and the use of cognitive distortions to justify this interest. If Mr. N does not come to this understanding, he is at risk of believing that his risk for re-offending has been eliminated by leaving Africa. An unfortunate effect of this false impression is that it could possibly undo the positive results of the interventions that have been taken thus far with his family with respect to family reunification, and threaten his continued participation in treatment. Mr. N needs to understand that his sexual arousal to girls can place him at risk in situations outside the family context, which he will need to monitor and manage on an ongoing basis. He also needs to be prepared to cope with this arousal and the resultant loss of control he is likely to experience, should it occur again in the future.

By this stage in treatment, Mr. N will understand his offense progression and the factors that may place him at risk for re-offending. These include periods of marital distance resulting from external factors, feelings of rejection and loneliness, cognitive distortions that are activated late in the offense progression, exposure to sexualized environments, sexual frustration and sexual interest that may or may not be deviant but that becomes problematic under certain circumstances, and sexual conservativism. He will also understand the relationship between his life goals, and the manner in which his life circumstances and tendency to subvert his desires led to sexual offending. Based on an understanding of the interplay among these factors, treatment then proceeds to assist Mr. N to develop adequate coping skills (internal conditions) and to enhance his existing skills to avoid offending, to manage situations (external conditions) that could trigger the desire to offend, and to achieve primary goods in non-offending ways.

From the perspective of the GLM, the promotion of approach goals (goods) can offset the chances of offending occurring. Thus, it is necessary to ensure that the avoidance of offending is achieved through the achievement of primary goods, particularly the offender's core commitments (i.e., overarching goods). For example, therapy should aim to equip Mr. N with the intimacy and emotional regulation skills (internal conditions) to establish a close relationship with his wife and to deal effectively with the inevitable strains that such a relationship entails. In addition, marital work and community interventions (external conditions) may be undertaken to ensure that Mr. N has the opportunity and support required to achieve these goals. Thus, providing him with the capabilities and opportunity to secure the goods of relatedness and emotional control via personally meaningful and realistic means ought to reduce his risk. It is important here to recall that Mr. N presents a low risk to re-offend, and that the objective of treatment is to maintain this low level of risk through strengthening his capacity to regulate his behavior in specific situations.

As noted above, Mr. N's goal is to avoid offending, and he has implemented effective strategies to achieve this goal. Thus, the primary focus of treatment is the reinforcement of these strategies, extinction of ineffective strategies, and the development of additional strategies to enhance his self-regulation capacity. In addition, a goal at this stage of treatment, as stated above, is to assist Mr. N to develop strategies to cope with stressors in his relationship with his wife and with the attendant negative emotional states arising in these situations, to challenge cognitive distortions, and to determine how he can effectively achieve primary goods and/or cope when these goods are not obtained.

In developing these strategies, Mr. N needs to acknowledge and commit to avoiding situations in which he would be exposed to abuse and to individuals supportive of abusive behavior. Given that Mr. N finds considerable gratification in his work, he needs to be assisted to delineate employment that would provide the same level of satisfaction but that would not place him at risk — that is, to find employment that capitalizes on his commitments to helping others and promoting a safer, fairer, and more decent world.

With respect to issues in his marital relationship, Mr. N will at this stage be aware of those times when he does not cope adequately with a loss of attention, intimacy and/or sexual activity in his relationship with his wife. He needs to develop the ability to monitor himself when he is experiencing negative emotional states, when he does not cope adequately, and when he feels that his needs are not being met. Part of this intervention involves accepting that it is natural in relationships to have an ebb and flow of attention and intimacy. As Mr. and Mrs. N have been in a relationship for an extended period of time, Mr. N will be able to identify those times in which he coped adequately with these periods. It is these skills he will use to cope in future, as well as new skills to both avoid and cope with these types of situations. For example, Mr. N may talk more openly with his wife about his feelings during these periods, he may take responsibility to plan activities together that do not involve other family members to ensure they spend time alone together, and he should ensure that he has an active social network in order to meet his needs and not to rely solely on his wife to do so. If required, Mr.

and Mrs. N can attend some minimal therapy together in order to learn to communicate effectively.

With respect to sexuality and pleasure more generally, Mr. N may need intervention in the area of core sexual beliefs in order to challenge his tendency to be sexually conservative and to ensure sexual satisfaction without guilt. Basic cognitive restructuring techniques, such as challenging rigid beliefs regarding appropriate sexual behavior and sexual expression, should be sufficient in Mr. N's case. For example, he will examine and challenge his views regarding masturbation and appropriate sexual fantasy such that he is aware that these are viable and acceptable means of sexual activity and gratification.

It is unlikely that Mr. N requires treatment targeting sexual arousal, such as arousal reconditioning interventions, unless it comes to light during treatment that he has committed other sexual offenses and/or that he engages in sexual fantasy of pre-pubescent or pubescent girls on a regular basis. As such, basic techniques such as *thought-stopping* and *incompatible responses* (Deffenbacher, 1996; Wolpe, 1990) are likely to be effective in aiding Mr. N to manage this arousal. Given his personal situation and his core pro-social beliefs, Mr. N may benefit simply from the development and reinforcement of a strategy by which he focuses on the negative consequences of offending, such as the loss of his family, employment, and/or his community standing, if he finds himself sexually aroused and/or fantasizing about girls.

Similarly, Mr. N will learn in treatment to challenge cognitive distortions that permit offending should he find himself in similar situations that pose a risk in the future. Primarily, he needs to learn to challenge the distortion that his daughter or other girls are sexually provocative. In doing so, the treatment provider assists him in generating other interpretations of innocuous behavior. For example, when his daughter giggles with one of her friends, he should generate such challenges as "they are sharing a childish secret", or "they are planning something fun to do together", or "girls can certainly be giggly and silly at times". Rehearsal and reinforcement of these types of challenges should result in these alternative thoughts being easily entrenched in Mr. N's case. In addition, Mr. N can draw upon existing challenges to this type of thinking. For example, he initially went to work in Africa to combat abuse against girls. Reiterating the reasons for which he knew this was abusive and became involved to stop this abuse represent pre-existing core beliefs that are incompatible with cognitive distortions. These are alternative thoughts that Mr. N can easily use, which have the further advantage of being consistent with his high level community goals. This aspect of treatment will "recruit" his commitment to social service work and justice, and motivate him to identify what he needs and wants in his life at these times. The construction of a list of challenges to problematic cognitions will also assist in the area of victim empathy and perspective-taking, which has heretofore been strength for Mr. N.

The final stage in treatment with Mr. N is to highlight the need for him to self-monitor on a regular basis to ensure that he is coping effectively with the situations identified above, that he is implementing effective strategies to prevent offending if such situations arise, and that he is adequately implementing his good life plan. The identification of the internal and external cues or triggers that could impair his ability to regulate his emotions and behavior are important to this process. This is particularly important when he is in the presence of his daughter, as well as other girls in the same age group. In addition, he should monitor the implementation of a lifestyle plan (i.e., a good lives plan) that builds on access to the primary human goods of relatedness, creativity, play, health, knowledge, spirituality, pleasure, work competency, inner peace (emotional regulation), and autonomy, and that also places emphasis on his particular commitments to helping other people without ignoring or downplaying his own needs. As we said above, this is an issue of autonomy in that Mr. N has tended to downplay his own concerns and interests on occasions, and to overemphasize them at other times.

While learning all of these new skills, it is essential that Mr. N be guided to practice his skills in a manner that results in success experiences, which will reinforce these new strategies and increase his self-efficacy and outcome expectations. The involvement of children's services in the family reunification process can be of assistance here, as can the involvement of his supportive family. He should begin the family reunification process by not being alone with his daughter until he demonstrates management of behavior in the areas identified above, a consistent and well-entrenched pattern of non-offending cognition and behavior, and resolution of the relationship issues and emotional coping associated with these difficulties. In addition, he should avoid being alone with pre-pubescent and pubescent girls, at least initially and perhaps over the long-term, again dependent upon the results of assessment of sexual interest and his demonstrated ability to manage his arousal and behavior and to achieve appropriate sexual gratification.

Maintenance and Supervision

As noted in Volume I, Mr. N successfully completed treatment while incarcerated and has been released to the community. He is undergoing follow-up with children's services and working toward family reunification. In the community, Mr. N would also participate in routine minimal supervision (e.g., via parole or probation services) designed to monitor that his risk to re-offend remains low, his functioning in his home relationships, any access to potential future victims, and the successful implementation of his good life plan. Assessment and treatment reports, including self-regulation plans, are a valuable source of information that can be used to identify any additional factors that may need to be monitored to manage the case, although these are likely to be minimal or nonexistent. Mr. N's supervision needs are likely to be minimal, although he would benefit from increased contact during the period of transition from prison to the community (i.e., the first three to six months), after which frequency of contact can be safely reduced when he demonstrates continued effective self-regulation.

Mr. N could benefit from participation in sexual offender maintenance treatment programming in the community as well. This would enable him to have professional support while using his non-offending strategies, as well as assistance should he encounter situations in which he did not cope effectively and to which he may respond negatively (e.g., the recurrence of sexual fantasy toward girls). As with supervision, frequency of contact can be higher during the initial stages of post-treatment maintenance immediately following his release from prison to the community. However, given his low risk to re-offend and the absence of numerous dynamic risk factors, long-term follow-up requirements in this area are minimal.

Given that Mr. N is involved with various agencies (i.e., children's services, probation or parole), collaboration between these agencies is essential to monitoring Mr. N's management of risk and to ensure appropriate responses to any situations in which he experiences a setback or indicates that he has not managed his behavior effectively. Balancing community safety, for example via disclosure, without setting up the offender for failure, requires careful consideration. Finally, Mr. N's family is pro-social and supports him both in general and specifically with respect to refraining from offending. This strong community support can be utilized by service agencies and providers to assist in monitoring Mr. N and ensuring his successful self-regulation and reintegration into the community.

One additional factor that must be considered in Mr. N's case is his employment, which has always been in a helping profession. This work clearly provides Mr. N with significant life and personal satisfaction and assists him to meet the good of community service and connectedness. It is recommended, therefore, that he be encouraged to continue in this line of work, but that he work with adults and not with children, and that he avoid work that would expose him to sexual or other abuse.

Chapter 7: Treatment implications for Offenders Following an Approach-automatic Pathway

Case Example Synopsis

Mr. O was convicted of two counts of indecent exposure following an incident in which he touched two girls on a train, during which he also masturbated to ejaculation. Following this, he disembarked from the train and approached another girl, with his penis exposed. Both on and off the train, he intended to have the girls perform fellatio on him. The girls boarded a bus and reported Mr. O's behavior. Prior to the offense, Mr. O had been drinking in a bar and had been interested in engaging in sexual activity with a woman who worked at the bar. He left when he decided that she was not interested. He had boarded the train knowing that there would be girls traveling on the train after school. After the girls reported his behavior to the bus driver, Mr. O proceeded to a liquor store to purchase some beer, where he was arrested. He admitted the offense to police, as well as several others that had not been reported.

In addition to the above-noted sexual offending behavior, Mr. O demonstrates symptomatology consistent with multiple co-morbid disorders that require evaluation and, likely, concurrent treatment. Specifically, it is noted that he was previously diagnosed with personality disorder (not specified in the file), depression, and an eating disorder that appears to be associated with long-term physical and sexual abuse committed against him by his father from the age of 8 to 16 years. Furthermore, he evidences behavior consistent with possible obsessive and/or obsessive-compulsive disorder, hypersexuality, schizotypal behavior, substance abuse, significant impairments in social judgment, and a lack of insight or judgment that is suggestive of the existence of major mental disorder. Finally, both his sexual offending behavior and substance abuse are known to be associated with his mood states, thereby suggesting not only the co-existence of multiple problem areas, but also the possibility that his sexual offending behavior may be solely or predominantly a result of undiagnosed mental disorder, or that these are linked in some as yet unidentified manner. Given the above, thorough evaluation and diagnosis is required in order to proceed with accurate risk assessment and appropriate treatment. In addition, Mr. O may also require pharmacological intervention for sexual arousal control prior to participation in a cognitive-behavioral intervention in order to be able to engage meaningfully in treatment.

Pathway Allocated: Approach-automatic

Within the self-regulation model of offending, the approach-automatic pathway is an acquisitive pathway characterized by poorly planned behavior that is impulsive or under-regulated. This behavior is initiated and carried out as a result of over-learned cognitive schema and/or sexual scripts. The individual following this pathway has an approach goal with respect to offending and does not attempt to refrain from offending or to inhibit his behavior. Behavior in the offense progression is considered automatic because it results from responses to internal and external stimuli based on well-entrenched scripts. These responses are typically habitual and not necessarily under the attentional control of the individual. When these individuals are faced with situations that trigger the desire to offend, they evidence a lack of restraint, lack of intentional control, and an absence of higher level goals. Planning of the offense is, at best, rudimentary. Individuals following this pathway may experience either positive or negative affective states associated with offending behavior, depending upon the individual. Positive emotional states experienced during the offense progression signal progress toward the offending goal. The post-offense evaluation is typically positive, as the approach goal has been achieved.

Mr. O is allocated to the approach-automatic pathway due to well-entrenched cognitive and sexual scripts that are activated by situational cues to which he responds in an automatic and unregulated manner. For example, Mr. O indicated that he realized that there would be girls boarding the train after school, and interpreted this as a possible situation in which he would receive sexual gratification, indicating an approach goal and situationally-activated sexual scripts. When encountering the girls on the train, Mr. O responded immediately by touching the girls and masturbating, and then approached them with his penis exposed. This offense sequence represents Mr. O's typical behavioral pattern of offending. Specifically, he reported exposing himself to girls on numerous occasions ("It must be thousands!") since the age of 15 years, as well as masturbation in this context. It is noted that, although Mr. O's behavior is impulsive and activated by situational cues (typical of this pathway), he also demonstrates some rudimentary planning. For example, he boarded the train knowing that there would be girls returning home from school.

It is noted that Mr. O's pathway allocation is, at this stage, provisional. Upon evaluation of Mr. O's mental status, as indicated above, this allocation should be revisited for confirmation.

Identified Risk Factors

Prior to treatment, risk factors are to be identified to evaluate Mr. O's risk for sexual re-offending and treatment needs based on static and dynamic factors. This assessment also provides information necessary for program matching and well as supervision.

The risk factors and resulting treatment targets described below focus solely upon Mr. O's sexual offending behavior and do not relate to his mental health needs. Furthermore, this risk assessment is provisional, as the nature and influence of mental disorder has not yet been evaluated or determined. Once such assessment has been conducted and Mr. O appropriately diagnosed, this risk assessment will be to be reviewed and revised as required.

Static Risk Factors.

- Single
- Prior sexual offenses
- Multiple prior sexual offense charges and convictions
- Convictions for non-contact sexual offenses
- Sexual offenses committed against unrelated victims
- Sexual offenses committed against stranger victims

Actuarial risk assessment measures assess risk to re-offend relative to other sexual offenders, using static factors empirically demonstrated to be predictive of recidivism. Using actuarial assessment of static risk (Static-99; Hanson & Thornton, 1999), Mr. O's risk factors place him at high risk to re-offend relative to other sexual offenders. Normative data for offenders falling into this category demonstrate a probability of sexual recidivism of 39%, 45%, and 52% over 5, 10, and 15 years, respectively.

In addition, Mr. O may present a risk for general criminal behavior. He has a criminal history for theft, primarily committed to enable him to purchase alcohol or drugs. This risk requires additional assessment and intervention as appropriate. He has no known history of nonsexual violence.

Dynamic Risk Factors/Treatment Targets. Dynamic risk factors are those factors empirically demonstrated to be predictive of sexual recidivism and which can be changed through intervention. The following treatment targets for Mr. O were based on case-specific factors as assessed against these dynamic risk factors, such as those described within the Stable 2000 (Hanson & Harris, 2004). As indicated above, this assessment is considered to be provisional until Mr. O's mental status has been thoroughly evaluated.

- Lack of significant positive social influences
- Intimacy/relationship deficits
- Problems with sexual self-regulation
- Problems with general self-regulation
- Attitudes supportive of sexual offending
- Cognitive distortions
- Substance abuse
- Access to potential victims
- Mental Disorder (Provisional)

Mr. O demonstrates significant deficits in key areas identified as dynamic risk factors for sexual offending. Although he does not appear to have significant negative social influences (e.g., criminal peers), he lacks a supportive, pro-social community support network. Mr. O also demonstrates intimacy deficits, including a lack of stable intimate relationships with adults and social rejection (possibly). Mr. O's most significant dynamic risk factors include problems with self-regulation, including both general and sexual self-regulation. With respect to the latter, Mr. O demonstrates significant sexual preoccupation and/or hypersexuality. His high sexual drive appears to lead him to seek out sexual gratification and expression when the opportunity presents itself, including public contexts, activated by situational cues. Although it is possible, he does not appear to be sexually gratified by the act of exposing himself per se. Instead, the presence of girls appears to activate his sexual urges, rather than triggering gratification of sexual desire via exposure.

Provisional Case Formulation

As indicated in Chapter 2, treatment within the GLM and SR models begins with a case formulation that is constructed on the basis of Mr. O's dynamic risk factors (vulnerability factors) and an understanding of the manner in which these are related to his offending, and is used to construct the treatment plan for Mr. O. This is achieved by considering whether the relationships between his pursuit of human goods and his offending are direct or indirect. In addition, Mr. O's overarching goods should be noted and their implications for his personal identity and subsequent plan for living evaluated. Because of the chronic, high risk nature of his behavior as well as his problems mood regulation and psychosocial functioning, the treatment plan for Mr. O will focus more on risk management than on attainment of primary goods, at least initially. Finally, the environment in which Mr. O is likely to be living should be taken into account and a practical action plan constructed.

It appears that Mr. O lacks the internal conditions (e.g., skills, self-efficacy beliefs) to effectively control his sexual desires and behavior, and also finds it difficult to regulate his impulses more generally (lack of access to the goods of autonomy and sexual pleasure). The link between primary goods and his offending appears to be a direct one in that Mr. O views deviant sexual activity as a way of obtaining pleasure as well as (possibly) social relatedness and connection. Recall that, frequently, individuals are not aware of the primary goods that motivate their offending and tend to confuse their stated goals with these (i.e., instrumental goods or means). It is possible that one of the problematic factors underlying his deviant sexual behavior is biological in nature, reflecting abnormal hormonal and neurotransmitter functioning. His inability to plan and achieve long-term goals means that his lifestyle tends to be rather chaotic and fragmented (i.e., his good life plan lacks consistency and coherency, and also reveals a lack of capabilities and resources). In addition, Mr. O lacks the emotional competency skills to effectively manage negative emotions and tends to use various substances improve his mood (does not have the good of inner peace). His relative social dislocation and lack of social networks means he is devoid of intimate relationships and a sense of belonging to a community (good of community). Overall, Mr. O presents as a rather chaotic, poorly functioning individual whose lack of social connectedness, subsequent antisocial attitudes, and general impulsivity are associated with a variety of psychological, social, and forensic problems.

Treatment needs to focus on providing the internal (e.g., skills training, self-efficacy, internal locus of control) and external (e.g., access to structured environments, resources, modeling) conditions required to achieve the goods of autonomy and social connectedness. In addition, his lack of social investment and concern for others could reflect antisocial attitudes and consequently it may be necessary to stress the prudential aspects of treatment more strongly than usual (i.e., self-interest). In terms of identity, one consequence of such a chaotic lifestyle is that Mr. O has a rather fractured, poorly developed sense of identity that tends to revolve around his sexual needs. A particularly important component of treatment will involve structuring his environment quite intensively and equipping Mr. O with the capacity to reflect on his lifestyle, goals, and behavior.

Intervention

As stated above, Mr. O has multiple and diverse treatment needs. Specifically, he suffers from co-occurring undiagnosed mental disorder, personality disorder, substance abuse, and sexual offending. As mentioned above, any intervention with Mr. O must take into consideration each of these issues based on comprehensive evaluation. What follows below are hypothesized specific interventions for an individual such as Mr. O following an approach-explicit pathway to offending. Although additional treatment needs are noted, the interventions described below target solely the sexual offending behavior and may need to be revised based on the outcome of additional evaluation.

With respect to sexual offending, Mr. O's core treatment need is sexual self-regulation. Specifically, he masturbates excessively and is unable to control or regulate the frequency and expression of his sexual behavior. He does not appear to evidence deviant sexual arousal in the classic sense. That is, although Mr. O indicated that he likes the reaction of the adolescent girls to whom he exposes himself, obtaining this reaction does not appear to his primary motivation for doing so. Rather, it appears that his primary motivation is his high sexual drive and his inability to regulate this drive. The good of sexual pleasure is sought inappropriately though exposure or is activated by situational cues in the environment, and his lack of ability to effectively plan his heterosexual encounters means that he tends to seek this out in public places. In addition, Mr. O is not able to function autonomously, and is somewhat captive to situational cues and influences. In short, he does not posses the internal and external conditions necessary to achieve important goods associated with his sexual needs. There is also a suggestion that his exhibitionism is a means of achieving admiration and desired intimacy, indicating problems with the pursuit of the good of relatedness.

Furthermore, although he admits to sexual fantasies of rape, he has not been known to act on these fantasies or to act out in a sexually violent, hands-on manner. In fact, there appear to be to incidents during which, when he could have acted out in a sexually violent manner via committing rape, that he did not do so, despite his obvious inability to self-regulate. For example, it would be expected that, if he were to act upon his rape fantasies, he would have done so against the woman in the bar who was not interested in him. In this situation, he simply left the bar, which is not what would be expected of an individual with a tendency to act on rape fantasies. As such, although Mr. O indicates multiple sexual preoccupations, he does not appear to be deviantly sexually aroused by one specific group of victims or solely by specific acts, such as rape or exhibitionism, although this may form part of his sexual pattern.

Although the core treatment need area for Mr. O is sexual self-regulation, this lack of sexual self-regulation appears to manifest itself when Mr. O experiences negative mood states and when he engages in substance use. In addition, Mr. O demonstrates concurrent deficits in the area of general self-regulation that are not necessarily associated with sexual offending or with deficits in sexual self-regulation, but which exist as separate deficits. The other dynamic risk factors indicated above appear to be consequential to both of these deficits. For example, it would be expected that Mr. O would lack significant positive social support persons and intimate relationships, given his day-to-day behavior. As such, while these dynamic risk factors will form part of treatment, they are deemed to be secondary in importance to general and sexual self-regulation. In other words, he experiences problems in achieving the goods of relatedness and community connectedness because of his sexually disinhibited behavior. However, it must be noted that despite the fact that Mr. O's social problems are *causally* dependent on his deviant sexual behavior, the social deficits from which he suffers are quite real and require specific targeting in treatment. It is also likely that his inability to manage negative emotions (and subsequent substance abuse) is also a direct consequence of the problems caused by his exhibitionistic behavior. In addition, some of these risk factors may be uniquely associated with mental disorder and may be resolved when this is successfully treated and managed.

Based on assessment and matching of static and dynamic risk factors, Mr. O would require a high intensity sexual offender treatment program (approximately 12 to 24 months), followed by maintenance programming. This intensity level reflects the presence of multiple risk factors and, particularly, the need in treatment to adequately assess and target his sexual self-regulation deficits and deviant sexual arousal. The treatment portion of intervention targets for change those case specific dynamic risk factors indicated above, which is described in detail below.

Following treatment, follow-up programming (i.e., maintenance), typically of longer duration than treatment but of fewer contact hours (e.g., several hours weekly or bi-monthly), is required, likely of long duration for Mr. O. This programming is designed to assist in the maintenance of skills acquired during treatment, rehearsal, reinforcement, and refinement of these skills and strategies, and entrenchment and internalization of strategies to manage risk to re-offend. While supervision provides the external sources of control over behavior that may be required for a short period of time, behavior that is managed by the individual himself (i.e., internal self-regulation) is more likely than external controls to be effective in managing risk over the long-term (Yates, 2003). In the case of Mr. O, maintenance programming will also integrate the various facets of the other interventions he will receive in addition to sexual offender treatment, such as the treatment of mental disorder, and will continue to coordinate with the various service providers working with him.

As Mr. O has received a non-custodial sentence, he will undergo treatment in the community, and requires high intensity supervision by parole or probation authorities concurrent with his treatment program.

Treatment

Prior to commencing cognitive-behavioral treatment, Mr. O will be evaluated to determine the requirement for pharmacological intervention. Specifically, Mr. O may require arousal-reducing medication in order to be able to successfully regulate his arousal during sex offender treatment and to reduce the frequency of masturbation. In addition, given the compulsive nature his sexual offending, Mr. O may require pharmacological intervention to manage this tendency, depending upon the results of his mental status evaluation. Finally, Mr. O may require pharmacological treatment for depression or mood disorder (Wettstein, 1998).

Treatment with Mr. O begins with behavioral contracting, by which he will agree not to expose himself during treatment and to seek the assistance of the treatment provider or his parole/probation officer should the desire to offend be triggered. Mr. O must also avoid those known specific situations that trigger the desire to offend, including particularly access to potential victims, as he is unable, at this time, to regulate his behavior. He will be provided with basic initial self-monitoring techniques (e.g., keeping daily logs to track the internal and external events that preceded his urge to masturbate or desire to offend and what strategies he uses in response to the urge; Heidt & Marx, 2003; Leahy, 2001) in order that he can become aware of his sexual arousal when this occurs. Results from ongoing self-monitoring and monitoring by treatment and supervision providers will be used in treatment to determine offense triggers and effective strategies to prevent offending over the long-term. In addition, basic techniques to control arousal will be provided to Mr. O. This will require some initial assessment to determine the most effective strategies to control arousal. In his case, simple techniques such as an elastic placed on his wrist which he snaps against his skin when he is aware that he has become sexually aroused, may be effective. He will be encouraged to masturbate if required, but must agree to limit this activity to his home as part of the behavioral contract. Given the influence of inadequate general, sexual, and mood self-regulation, Mr. O is unlikely to be able to implement and to benefit from more sophisticated cognitive techniques at this initial stage of treatment, unless medication management has been successfully implemented. If possible, Mr. O will be linked with community support to assist in monitoring and avoiding offending. A Circle of Support (Wilson & Prinzo, 2001; Wilson et al., 2003) is likely to be of particular value to his risk management and treatment participation. Finally, because of its disinhibitory effects, Mr. O must avoid substance use during treatment, and this will form part of the behavioral contract with him. Mr. O must receive consistent positive reinforcement from treatment providers and probation/parole staff when he successfully complies with the behavioral contract as well as when he implements effective avoidance and self-regulation strategies. Failure to adhere to the behavioral contract must be addressed, and plans made to increase compliance.

Generally, individuals following an approach-automatic pathway do not share the treatment provider's goal of ceasing sexual offending. As such, Mr. O is unlikely, at least initially, to be amenable to treatment and is likely to be resistant to the idea of change. He appears to be in the precontemplative stage of change (DiClemente, 1991; Prochaska & DiClemente, 1982; 1986) and has approach goals with respect to offending. As stated above, these are likely to involve the pursuit of sexual pleasure, relatedness, and emotional relief. Despite numerous arrests and convictions, Mr. O does not believe he has a problem and does not believe his behavior is abusive or harmful to others. However, he does state that he believes that rape is wrong, which may serve as a starting point in treatment with Mr. O. This may increase his engagement with treatment and to allow him to consider that his sexual offending behavior is inappropriate. In addition, based on his own personal history, including extensive sexual and other abuse committed against him by his father, Mr. O has well-entrenched cognitive and sexual scripts and attitudes that support non-contact sexual offending, of which he is unaware.

The aim of treatment in these early stages is to present information designed to increase awareness that he has a problem that must be addressed. It is insufficient to assume that, because he has been convicted, Mr. O will come to realize that his behavior is problematic. Thus, awareness of the problem must be created. This is particularly evident in Mr. O's case, as he has been convicted on previous occasions, and readily admits that he has engaged in this type of behavior on numerous occasions.

Given the above, the first stage in treatment with Mr. O is to raise his awareness that his behavior is offensive, to determine his higher level life goals (of which he is also unaware) and to create in him consideration of behavioral change. Various treatment methods are available to assist the treatment provider in commencing this process. As part of the behavioral contract described above, Mr. O will have begun self-monitoring of the urges and desire to offend, and the internal and external states that trigger these desires. The treatment facilitator can analyze the results of self-monitoring with Mr. O in order to uncover the specific primary goods he seeks via offending. The treatment facilitator can support him to see how treatment can provide him alternatives, which likely will be more successful, to achieve these higher level goals. The treatment provider can also feed back to Mr. O the results of risk and other assessments to illustrate the manner in which his current responses are incompatible with his achievement of his higher level goals of autonomy, social connection, peace, and sexual pleasure. First, the treatment provider can discuss with Mr. O the results of the pre-treatment assessment, including his high risk rating. During this process, Mr. O is asked to indicate the reasons for which, in his view, he is considered to be high risk. He should be able to generate problem areas such as his high frequency of offending and masturbating, and approaching adolescent girls in public. Mr. O is then asked to generate the reasons for which such behavior is problematic. *Do other people masturbate and experience sexual feelings? How do other people obtain sexual pleasure without getting in trouble with the law? Why do other people view his behavior as a problem? Does he view this behavior as (potentially) problematic? How does what he does differ from people who are not arrested for sexual offending? How is his behavior different from people who are not referred for sex offender treatment? Are there other ways that he can meet his sexual needs that won't result in legal consequences?*

A cost-benefit (Cherry, 2005; Leahy, 2001; Miller & Rollnick, 1991) analysis can also assist Mr. O in understanding the negative consequences of his behavior. Questions of this nature and the cost-benefit analysis are designed to have Mr. O begin to think about those aspects of his life and specific behaviors that he would like to change, as they are related to his higher goals. Mr. O has himself stated that he sometimes feels that he is not in control, a statement that can be explored in order for him to uncover the reasons for which he feels out of control and to delineate those behaviors over which he would like to exercise control. *What are his ultimate (higher level) goals in life? What would his ideal (good) life look like? How does non-offending enhance these life goals? How can treatment help in achieving these goals? How can developing new skills help him overcome his sense of failure and worthlessness and result in the achievement of personally valued goals (i.e., goods)? How would life be different if he felt he had more control?* Not only does this process assist in engagement with treatment, it can also function to create a positive expectancy for treatment, commitment to treatment goals, and the development of an avoidance goal with respect to offending. Once an avoidance goal is established, Mr. O can begin to learn strategies to achieve this goal and can importantly begin to seek positive life goals that will reduce his need to seek such goods as sexual pleasure through indecent exposure and other offending behaviors. Mr. O's commitment to an avoidance goal is expected to be variable. As a consequence, ongoing discussion and reinforcement of his positive life goals and his alternative methods to achieve them must be undertaken at various points during treatment.

The objective is to increase Mr. O's level of awareness and to assist him in realizing that he has engaged in problematic behavior, to recognize that his offending behavior has resulted in negative consequences for him, and that it has interfered with his life goals. The aim is also to enhance Mr. O's amenability to treatment via the framing of treatment as a process by which he can improve his life. Because he is in the precontemplative stage of change, it will not be useful to attempt to convince Mr. O that he has a "problem". Rather, once Mr. O has identified problem areas and life goals on which he would like to work, he will be more amenable to treatment. Although low at this stage, Mr. O's motivation to change his behavior and his level of engagement with treatment will increase later in treatment. The techniques indicated above are designed to ensure that Mr. O begins to engage in the treatment process.

Once Mr. O has identified the problem areas and good life goals on which he would like to work, the treatment provider establishes with him mutually agreed-upon goals for the treatment process, based on these target areas. In Mr. O's case, his goals are likely to be significantly different from those of the treatment provider. For example, Mr. O may indicate such goals as "obtaining a sexual relationship" or "getting his needs met without being arrested and charged". While it is obvious that these goals are not yet fully inclusive of the overall goal of treatment of ultimately not offending, the challenge for the treatment provider is to utilize these goals in such a manner that they ultimately become inclusive of this treatment goal. The treatment provider will utilize Mr. O's stated goals as the initial basis of treatment, as well as establish his larger, good life goals. These goals will be reviewed periodically throughout treatment, so they may be successively refined. It is necessary to distinguish between the primary goods underlying Mr. O's stated goals from the goals themselves (e.g., obtaining a sexual relationship with a girl). For example, sex with a girl may be a means by which Mr. O seeks intimacy, emotional relief, or simply pleasure. These primary goods are quite acceptable; it is the means that are used to achieve them (i.e., via sexual activity with girls or exposing himself) that are problematic. Helping Mr. O understand just what he is seeking through sex with girls does two things: (a) it helps to clarify his motives, and (b) it can motivate him to acquire the capabilities and resources to achieve his overarching goals in socially acceptable ways.

It is important to note that Mr. O's engagement with treatment is also likely to be inhibited by the chronic vulnerability factors that lead to his offending behavior, in addition to his lack of awareness that his behavior is problematic. Specifically, he is likely to find it challenging to explore his offending behavior in detail, as a result of viewing this behavior as non-problematic, and is likely to become defensive when it is suggested that his behavior is deviant and offensive. Should this occur, the treatment provider will need to change strategies in order for Mr. O to continue to progress in treatment.

The next phase of treatment with Mr. O consists of raising his awareness of the chronic factors that place him at risk to offend. This involves having him describe his history, including all of his undetected offending behavior, using the nine-phase self-regulation model. This task can be described as his opportunity to explain his life to assist the treatment provider to understand what he has experienced, as well as for him to identify those factors in his life which have left him vulnerable to engage in sexual offending. In addition to raising awareness, this disclosure exercise also allows both Mr. O and the treatment provider to understand clearly the links between his life history, personal goals, chronic vulnerability factors, dynamic risk factors, and the manner in which particular life events or situations trigger the offense process and the desire to offend.

As noted previously, Mr. O was severely abused and neglected between the ages of eight and sixteen by his father, both physically and sexually. The abuse stopped when he left home at the age of sixteen. Undoubtedly, this abuse has had a significant impact on the development of Mr. O's sexual offending behavior, as well as significant psychological consequences. These experiences are likely to be elucidated by Mr. O during this disclosure exercise. Mr. O should be referred to specialized psychological therapy for this issue. Although the sex offender therapist will likely need to take some intervention in order to assist him to cope with negative emotional reactions that may arise, Mr. O will not receive intervention for this issue in the context of sex offender treatment. Given the nature and extent of the abuse committed against Mr. O, and his reaction to this abuse, it is essential that he participate in therapy for this with a trained therapist who specializes in victimization and its treatment. Furthermore, prolonged or in-depth discussion of this victimization during sex offender treatment should be avoided.

Depending on Mr. O's response to this disclosure exercise, prior to proceeding to the analysis of offending, the treatment provider may revisit his initial goals for treatment and his good life goals, in order to refine these further and to reinforce his commitment to obtaining primary goods by appropriate means. This is done if Mr. O has gained some insight from the disclosure exercise, as indicated by statements on his part acknowledging problematic behavior. If this has not occurred, treatment then proceeds to the analysis of the offense progression and revisits treatment goals at a later time.

Mr. O has a long and frequent history of sexual offending. In analyzing his offense behavior, the aim is not to obtain the specific details of each instance of offending. Rather, the aim is to identify consistent behavioral and cognitive patterns in order to later develop effective strategies to prevent re-offending. The nine-phase self-regulation model will be particularly useful in Mr. O's case, and he will work through this model in concrete detail. The first step is to determine those life events and circumstances that trigger the desire to offend and that initiate the offense progression. In Mr. O's case, as indicated above, he demonstrates numerous predisposing factors, including mental disorder, personality disorder, substance abuse, deficits in both general and sexual self-regulation, and negative mood that may result from mental disorder. His sexual offending behavior results from his lack of sexual self-regulation, hypersexuality, and possible compulsive disorder. It appears Mr. O's offending is activated by situational cues that activate overlearned sexual scripts he is unable to manage, which in turn trigger negative mood and substance abuse – factors that disinhibit his behavior. As a consequence of these predisposing factors and his sexual self-regulation difficulties, he evidences some cognitive distortions and has developed rape fantasies. Some dynamic risk factors indicated above, including intimacy deficits and social isolation, appear to have both influenced the development of his sexual offending behavior and to be consequences of this behavior. Finally, during post-offense phases, Mr. O's post-offense evaluation and attitude toward future offending are likely to be positive, particularly since he receives powerful positive reinforcement for behavior in post-offense stages, including masturbation to ejaculation.

It is unlikely that all of the circumstances which trigger offending can be identified, given the high frequency of his offending behavior. Similarly, it is unlikely that Mr. O will be able to develop specific strategies for each of the specific multiple situations that trigger the desire to offend. However, given available information, Mr. O can develop strategies to minimize the influence of his chronic vulnerability and dynamic risk factors, and to resolve specific issues associated with these factors in order that he can achieve his higher life goals. Because Mr. O is receiving treatment in the community, the analysis of his offending behavior will include those factors which currently trigger the desire to offend.

Because his lack of sexual self-regulation results on some occasions from under-regulation due to negative mood and/or substance abuse, Mr. O needs to recognize these as triggers of his desire to offend in that negative mood is often prompted by his lifestyle and behaviors that do not facilitate his achievement of his primary goals of connectedness, autonomy, and pleasure. As indicated previously, he requires treatment for substance abuse and possibly for depression. These interventions should assist in minimizing the occurrence of negative mood and substance use, thereby reducing their impact on his sexual under-regulation. Medication management for both depression and sexual drive are likely to be an integral part of ongoing intervention with Mr. O. Thus, during the analysis of his offending behavior, Mr. O needs to come to an understanding of these factors in order that he may develop strategies to cope in these areas later in treatment.

Also during the analysis of his offending behavior, Mr. O explores his perceptions and interpretations of events surrounding his behavior, prior to, during, and following offending, and any rudimentary planning, decision-making and selection of strategies. For example, during the present offense, Mr. O indicated that he knew the school girls against whom he offended would be on the train. At this stage, he made the decision to offend, albeit impulsively. Although his behavior is under-regulated, he can still determine the reasons for which he made the decision to offend and can develop strategies to minimize the likelihood of future offending. In Mr. O's case, it is clear that he will need to avoid situations in which he has access to potential future victims. Because he has a clear target group of victims (adolescent girls, typically between the ages of twelve and sixteen) and only offends during the day, he can develop clear strategies to avoid access to potential future victims. For example, he can ensure that he avoids going out during the day during those hours when schoolchildren would be accessible, that he only goes out during these hours with a support person, or that he is otherwise occupied during these hours, such as at work or school.

During the analysis of offending and strategy development, Mr. O needs to identify that, in addition to resulting from under-regulation, his behavior is automatic in that it is based on well-entrenched cognitive and behavioral scripts that are activated by situational cues. Once this is done, Mr. O can learn to identify the sequence of his behavior and cognition in order to break down its automatic nature.

That is, Mr. O will delineate the concrete triggers and actions he takes in response to these triggers, in order to understand that he can exercise control and reduce the impulsive nature of his responses. This is accomplished in treatment by having Mr. O examine the temporal sequence of events and actions in a step-by-step manner.

As indicated above, Mr. O has a long history of offending behavior, for which a clear pattern can likely be detected. Through the analysis of offending, he will come to understand this pattern. Mr. O typically offends on several occasions over a period of several days, after which he ceases for a period of time. It will be essential not only to detect this pattern, but also to determine the reasons for which he ceases offending and the strategies he uses to avoid offending during these periods. If sexual offending is exclusively or predominantly compulsive, he may stop offending because he has injured himself physically or has achieved sufficient reduction in anxiety levels. In this case, medication and treatment of this disorder will assist in reducing the probability of offending. Alternatively, if Mr. O is able, during these non-offending periods, to successfully implement strategies to regulate himself sexually, treatment will build upon, augment, and reinforce these existing skills. These existing skills and cognitions can be identified through a series of questions. *Given that he appears to only offend during the day, what specifically does he do during the evening to manage his arousal and to regulate his mood? Are there effective strategies that he uses at this time that can be applied to his entire day? What other things does he do that give him pleasure, that provide him with a sense of social connectedness, etc.?*

In addition to his offending behavior, Mr. O's analysis needs to include the nature and content of the sexual fantasies he reports (rape), and the relationship of these, if any, to his offending behavior. He reports that he has not acted upon these fantasies. If true, minimal intervention will likely be required to develop and rehearse appropriate and equally satisfying sexual fantasy material. It is also necessary to identify the themes inherent in these fantasies as they can point to enduring concerns associated with the unsuccessful achievement of primary goods. For example, offenders may believe that their status as males (i.e., social standing) has been unfairly impugned by females and may seek to establish their independence by raping someone; effectively a grievance driven rape related to issues of autonomy and "community" connectedness (typically a deviant subgroup). Uncovering these themes will enable the therapies and Mr. O to better understand both goods sought and the nature of the specific intervention that will be required.

As Mr. O does not demonstrate a high level of insight into his offending behavior at the onset, information gathering needs to be done in a non-threatening manner in order to facilitate understanding and to minimize resistance. For these types of offenders, inappropriate techniques can result in defensiveness. The treatment provider must assist Mr. O to evaluate his problem areas and deficits in a non-threatening manner to ensure he does not abandon treatment. Techniques that can optimize learning and decrease resistance include open-ended questioning, reflection of content and affect, allowing the offender time to generate information and links, and providing reinforcement for successful discovery and skills rehearsal (Beck, 1995; Fernandez, Shingler, & Marshall, 2006; Leahy, 2001; Segrin, 2003). While the treatment provider should lead the offender in this process, it will be more effective to allow him to reach an understanding on his own (although guided by the therapist), rather than providing him with our "expert" interpretations.

It is important to note that, in Mr. O's case, treatment can trigger sexual arousal. For example, because Mr. O evidences a high sexual drive and lacks sexual self-regulation, disclosure of offending behavior or fantasy material can result in arousal to this material during disclosure. As such, the treatment provider needs to be attentive to this development, and to ensure that Mr. O has managed this arousal prior to leaving the treatment session and returning to the community. In addition, if Mr. O does become aroused during treatment, the exercise is halted, and arousal management is implemented before continuing.

By this stage in treatment, Mr. O will be familiar with his risk factors for offending, will have an understanding of the goods he seeks to achieve via offending, and will have been learning and implementing a variety of self-regulation skills. Following analysis of his offending behavior, treatment revisits his initial (or revised) treatment goals in order to further refine these and to link these with his higher order life goals. In addition, both at this time and throughout treatment, the therapist and Mr. O determine those self-regulation strategies that are effective and additional strategies he can adopt at this time, particularly if progress in mood management and arousal control has been made. This also includes reviewing the behavioral contract and revising this to include additional strategies and/or to remove strategies that have been ineffective. *Is he able to successfully avoid situations that place him at risk to offend? On those instances in which he has not been successful, what went wrong and how can he be successful in these types of situations in the future? Is his community support (e.g., Circle of Support) effective and helpful? Has he made progress in mental health and substance abuse interventions?* The sex offender treatment provider will collaborate with mental health and substance abuse providers to integrate treatment strategies and to assess and enhance risk management.

With respect to his specific deficits, there are numerous additional skills development techniques that can be applied with Mr. O. Specifically, to target general self-regulation deficits, Mr. O is assisted to develop basic social skills in multiple life areas, such as planning, communication, and establishing relationships. With respect to coping with negative mood and/or depression, in addition to medication management, Mr. O will learn to implement basic strategies to monitor his mood and to take concrete steps (such as contacting his therapist, parole/probation officer, or other community support person) when he experiences depressive or negative mood states. Mr. O can be taught to identify those negative emotions that trigger difficulties and to monitor the intensity of those emotions using a concrete scale that helps him to identify when he is experiencing problems (e.g., illustrating the building of negative emotions using a traffic light analogy, with "green" representing few or no problems, "yellow" representing the need to examine life circumstances because problems are emerging, and "red" indicating the need to cease all activity and seek out assistance from the therapist, supervisor, or other support person). Mr. O will be instructed, at least initially, to take a "time-out" (Friman & Finney, 2003; Leahy, 2001) when his mood is deteriorating. During this time-out, he will be encouraged not to rely on his historical strategies of fantasy and masturbation to make himself feel better or to engage in rumination. Rather, he will be taught basic thought stopping and distraction techniques (Deffenbacher, 1996; Wolpe, 1990) and to ask for help so that he will be able to seek assistance from positive supports in his life during these periods. When he is able to do so, he will begin to implement cognitive change strategies by which he intervenes when he experiences these mood states.

Cognitive and behavioral interventions that are likely to be effective with Mr. O include continued ongoing self-monitoring (Heidt & Marx, 2003; Leahy, 2001) and the immediate implementation of negative consequences when he experiences the desire to offend. It is expected that Mr. O's risky self-talk will be primarily his justification for continued offending behavior because of his distortion that there is no victim harm. Significant effort will need to be placed on assisting him to develop thoughts (self-talk) that will serve to counter these distortions and that will help him obtain a different perspective. He will need to be guided to see that harm is not only a consequence of direct physical contact and to develop personally relevant counter statements that he can use. It can be as basic as developing self-talk by which he tells himself *"I can only masturbate at home", "the only time I can do anything sexual is when I have permission to do this", and "permission can only be given by adults, not girls".* As indicated above, Mr. O will need to continue to avoid situations that place him at risk, and to prevent access to potential victims. If he is unable to do so and is unable to implement effective self-regulation strategies, he will agree to contact a member of his treatment or supervision team, community support, police, doctor, or hospital if his risk to offend is imminent. At the same time, he is encouraged to engage in self-talk that focuses on the manner in which offending interferes with his life goals and obtaining primary goods, and on using self-talk that facilitates their acquisition.

Because Mr. O's sexual experience is limited and is predominantly associated with his own offending behavior as well as the sexual abuse committed by his father, basic sex education may be useful in order to assist him to develop non-abusive sexuality. This will enable him to grasp the multiple goods associated with sex and the importance of sometimes seeking to secure these goods via nonsexual means (e.g., intimacy or emotional regulation).

In the area of victim empathy, Mr. O will be assisted to develop basic perspective-taking (Marshall et al., 1999; Yates et al., 2000) to counter his belief that his behavior is not harmful to others. Part of perspective-taking will include educating him about consent, boundaries and respectful social interactions. In treatment he can explore creating alternative perspectives to various scenarios. At the very minimum, he must learn that lack of reaction does not mean permission to expose or touch. Any time he engages with someone in sexual activity it can only be in private places with explicit consent. These interventions are related to the goods of autonomy, social relatedness, and community connectedness. Mr. O will ideally learn that adult intimate relationships require mutual respect and competence to consent to sexual activity. They occur between people of equal standing and power, and ought to benefit each partner.

Because he is under-regulated, Mr. O will benefit from establishing structure in his daily life; essentially ensuring that the appropriate external conditions for implementing a good lives plan are instituted. He will be assisted to develop a schedule to which he must adhere. Mr. O has a great deal of unstructured time and is hypersexual, leading him to spend much of his days fantasizing, masturbating, and engaging in offending. As he starts to learn to regulate himself, he must fill his time with satisfying and productive activities, as well as allowing himself time to continue to meet his sexual needs in appropriate manner. How he fills this schedule will be contingent upon those goods for which he is striving. This may involve, for example, returning to school or finding work, which would assist him in working toward the goods of knowledge, mastery, creativity, and community.

It is expected that behavior change will not happen immediately or without difficulty. In order to effectively manage Mr. O's risk to re-offend, agreement among the treatment and supervision team will be established with respect to intervention for lapses. These management strategies will be developed in collaboration with Mr. O and will form part of the behavioral contract to which he has agreed. This will involve immediate assessment of acute risk. If risk is critical and offending is imminent, the team will agree to provide immediate service to him or to contact appropriate authorities or support persons, depending upon the situation and the immediate risk. If he has experienced a lapse but risk to offend is not imminent, the treatment team will have agreed upon an approach by which therapeutic intervention is taken with Mr. O. In this intervention, the team will explore the factors that prompted the trigger and will analyze with Mr. O those aspects of his self-regulation strategies that are not working or that he needs to practice or re-initiate. Mr. O would be well-served by engaging in daily self-monitoring (e.g., via continuing to keep a log; Heidt & Marx, 2003; Leahy, 2001), and the primary activity that he monitors at any given time would be the strategy for which he needs to develop more competence. If he needs to develop alternative skills and strategies, this too would be identified during review of his self-monitoring exercise. Mr. O would also be guided to assess how competent he feels he is in managing risky thinking, feelings and situations. The ultimate goal is to ensure that Mr. O has developed a skill set that allows him to work toward his goods in a pro-social manner. The intervention team also needs to ensure reinforcement of disclosure by Mr. O of the desire to offend. Such disclosure indicates that Mr. O continues to be engaged with the treatment process and is attempting to manage his behavior. If he ceases to disclose fantasy, lapses, or a desire to offend, this is likely to indicate that his risk to re-offend has increased and that increased intervention is required.

Maintenance and Supervision

Because he is serving his sentence in the community, Mr. O would also participate in frequent and high intensity supervision (i.e., via parole or probation services) simultaneously with sex offender and other treatment interventions.

Mr. O is likely to require long-term treatment prior to moving to the maintenance phase of intervention, which will also be of high intensity. Treatment should cease and maintenance begin only when he demonstrates significant ability to self-monitor and self-regulate for an extended period of time across multiple circumstances, and when it is clear that he is effectively implementing his good life plan.

In the case of Mr. O, the maintenance phase of treatment will, in some respects, be similar to the treatment phase of intervention. Mr. O will continue ongoing self-monitoring as described above, and maintenance will continue to monitor and enhance the effectiveness of his self-regulation strategies. His ability to monitor and effectively cope with negative mood and substance abuse will continue to be a target in the maintenance phase, as would compliance with his medication management regime (if applicable). Behavioral contracting (as described above) will also continue until Mr. O demonstrates that this is no longer required by effectively implementing self-regulation strategies. Finally, maintenance will continue to monitor and assist Mr. O in implementing his good life plan.

Chapter 8: Treatment Implications for Offenders Following an Approach-explicit Pathway

Case Example Synopsis

Mr. B is a forty-year old man convicted of six counts of sexual assault for offenses committed over a period of eight years against one victim, a boy between the ages of ten and eighteen years. He pleaded guilty to these offenses. Mr. B met the boy when he was working as a handyman for the boy's family and offended against him progressively via fondling, having the boy masturbate and perform fellatio on him, and forcing anal sexual intercourse. He was able to maintain the abuse via threats that the boy would not be believed if he reported the assaults. Mr. B was previously arrested when he was nineteen years of age for sexual assault of a fourteen-year-old boy, and when he was twenty-six years of age for sexual assault against a teenaged boy. He participated in prison-based treatment and was released at the age of thirty-two. While in prison, Mr. B coerced sexual activity from other inmates in exchange for helping them in prison.

Pathway Allocated: Approach-explicit

Within the self-regulation model of offending, the approach-explicit pathway is characterized as an acquisitional pathway in which self-regulation is intact. Individuals following this pathway have approach goals with respect to offending and their behavior is adequately regulated. They do not desire or attempt to avoid sexual offending and do not offend as a function of under-regulation or mis-regulation. Rather, these individuals explicitly plan their offenses.

Typically, a number of approach goals are evident in their offenses, such as attempts to establish intimate relationships (e.g., via grooming victims), re-establishing a sense of autonomy, sexual pleasure, the creative manipulation of another person, or simply novelty seeking. Similarly, although the individual may evidence some deficits in functioning or skills, such as intimate relationships, these deficits do not represent the primary dynamic of sexual offending. Rather, offense goals are associated with core beliefs that support sexual offending, and these individuals do not attempt to refrain from offending. In fact, they actively and explicitly utilize strategies in order to offend. Core beliefs may be associated with positive affect when they are concerned with the self and relationships, or negative affect when concerned with feelings associated with being wrongfully or unfairly treated. Post-offense affect and evaluation for individuals following this pathway is typically positive, as they have achieved their goal.

Mr. B is allocated to the approach-explicit pathway, due to his approach goal to offending and his explicit and planned behavior to achieve this goal. He did not attempt to refrain from offending and sought out his victims via his employment, choosing to work in settings in which he knew he would have access to, and would be alone with, children. He specifically targeted vulnerable children, whom he described as "misfits, the lonely ones who would spend time around me," and whose trust he believed he could easily gain. Mr. B had also targeted boys in his school when he was younger, where he was sexually abused by the priests running the school. He reported a sense of power associated with abusing other boys, which he regarded as teaching them about life. During his first prison term, Mr. B was similarly sexually assaulted by an older inmate, whom he regarded as a "protector", and later began to target younger inmates to "educate" them about prison life, charging them his rightful "fee" for their protection. He regarded these activities as consensual. He does not regard his sexual abuse of boys (both current and prior) as harmful or abusive. In fact, he believes that he is doing them a service or getting what is rightfully his. From the perspective of the GLM, he believes he is appropriately seeking the goods of life, agency, pleasure, and relationships.

Identified Risk Factors

Prior to treatment, risk factors are identified to evaluate Mr. B's risk for sexual re-offending based on static and dynamic factors. This assessment provides information necessary for program matching, developing treatment targets, and supervision.

Static Risk Factors. Actuarial risk assessment measures risk to re-offend relative to other sexual offenders, using static factors empirically demonstrated to be predictive of recidivism. Using actuarial assessment of static risk (Static-99; Hanson & Thornton, 1999), Mr. B's assessed risk factors place him at a moderate-high risk to re-offend relative to other sexual offenders. Normative data for offenders falling into this category demonstrate a probability of sexual recidivism of 39%, 45%, and 52% over 5, 10, and 15 years, respectively.

- Single/never married
- Prior charges/convictions for sexual offenses
- Sexual offenses committed against unrelated victims
- Sexual offenses committed against male victims
- Recidivism following treatment completion

Mr. B is unlikely to present a risk for violent or general criminal behavior. He has no history of nonsexual violence or other criminality, nor is there evidence of attitudes supportive of crime or identification or association with pro-criminal others.

Dynamic Risk Factors/Treatment Targets. Dynamic risk factors are those factors empirically demonstrated to be predictive of sexual recidivism and which can be changed through intervention. The following treatment targets for Mr. B were based on case-specific factors as assessed against these dynamic risk factors, such as those described within the Stable 2000 (Hanson & Harris, 2004).

- Lack of significant positive social influences
- Intimacy/relationship deficits
- Lack of concern for others
- Attitudes supportive of sexual offending
- Cognitive distortions
- Deviant sexual interests/preference

Mr. B reports that he has offended sexually on multiple occasions. He explicitly targets and manipulates his victims in order to receive sexual gratification from his preferred target group. That is, Mr. B has deviant sexual preferences for prepubescent and pubescent boys. His job as a handyman allows him access to schools, community centers, and private homes, where he can offend. He takes advantage of his work situation in order to befriend children for the ultimate purpose of sexual activity. He explicitly targets boys whom he regards as vulnerable. As such, he clearly indicates deviant sexual preference and makes use of explicit strategies to manipulate situations to facilitate offending.

Mr. B was sexually abused by several priests at school at the age of ten years. Under threat, he was told not to disclose the offenses. According to Mr. B, these priests introduced him to other boys with whom he engaged in sexual activity, after which Mr. B began seeking out other boys of his own accord. He indicated that he believed he was "doing them a favor by showing them what real life was like", and that this made him feel powerful. Mr. B has also coerced sexual activity from other inmates when he was incarcerated as an adult, explicitly to meet his own needs. He regards these as consensual adult relationships. As such, Mr. B demonstrates well-entrenched attitudes supportive of sexual offending, which he appears to have learned from both his own victimization. These attitudes appear to have been developed and reinforced since an early age.

As a result of these entrenched attitudes, Mr. B does not regard his sexual offending as problematic or believe his sexual arousal to boys is inappropriate. Rather, he views this as simply a normal feature of the relationships he establishes with his victims (in his mind, consenting partners). He explicitly approaches offending and directly seeks certain goals via the sexual abuse of boys (e.g., pleasure, relatedness, mastery, etc.).

As indicated above, one of Mr. B's dynamic risk factors is the presence of cognitive distortions. However, these distortions are simply reflective of his attitudes and belief system that are supportive of offending. Although these will be targeted in treatment, the primary focus is one of attitude change, which must occur prior to targeting the distortions.

Another identified dynamic risk factor for Mr. B is lack of concern for others. This is evident in his belief that his behavior is not harmful to others and that it may, in fact, be beneficial to them. As such, he lacks empathy and the ability to take the perspective of others. This is also reflective of Mr. B's overall worldview that the world is a dangerous place in which there are winners and losers. Consequently, he will take that which makes him feel powerful, which he understands as simply the way of the world. This worldview also manifests as a strong sense of entitlement, which allows Mr. B to take that to which he feels entitled and that others must accept this as part of the harsh reality. One place where this attitude is evident is in Mr. B's interactions with other prison inmates. Given this worldview and the manner in which he treats others, it is not surprising that Mr. B also has deficits in intimate relationships, thereby indicating the existence of this dynamic risk factor, which is also reflective of his inability to obtain the primary good of intimacy.

While serving a prison term, Mr. B successfully completed sexual offender treatment of approximately one year's duration, followed by follow-up programming while on probation. However, during treatment, he did not feel he was similar to other sexual offenders, did not believe that he had coerced sexual activity from boys when he was younger or from other inmates, and did not view himself as a sexual offender. He subsequently re-offended, however, although he stated that some time has passed since receiving treatment and committing the current offense.

Provisional Case Formulation

As indicated in Chapter 2, treatment within the GLM and SR models begins with a case formulation that is constructed on the basis of Mr. B's dynamic risk factors (vulnerability factors) and an understanding of the manner in which these are related to his offending, and is used to construct the treatment plan for Mr. B. This is achieved by considering whether the relationship between his pursuit of human goods and his offending is direct or indirect. In addition, Mr. B's overarching goods should be noted, and their implications for his personal identity and subsequent plan for living identified. Finally, the environment in which Mr. B is likely to be living should be taken into account and a practical action plan constructed that considers this environment.

Mr. B has a long history of sexual offending following his own abuse by priests. He believes that sex between adults and children is normal as long as it is not coercive and does not involve violence. It appears that there is a direct link between certain primary goods and Mr. B's extensive history of sexual offending. His view that sex is a legitimate aspect of "educating" boys suggests that he sees himself as a mentor figure or teacher. The sexual activity is a means of cementing this relationship and is also a form of payment for his "expertise". This suggests that he has difficulty obtaining the goods of intimacy, agency, autonomy, safety, and friendship. He seeks these directly via his abusive behavior. This is likely to be a consequences of his own early developmental history with respect to sex, abuse, and power, and his long-standing attitudes which developed as a result of these experiences. Furthermore, it seems that Mr. B uses sex with boys as a means of meeting his intimacy needs and he typically takes considerable time to build (or groom) vulnerable individuals. He sees their vulnerability as indicators that they require his support and help, and consequently regards them as suitable sexual objects. In other words, Mr. B's cognitive distortions stem from his beliefs that he has a positive influence on those boys he chooses to "educate" about the nature of the world. A related issue concerns his view of the world as dangerous place and hence the importance of seeking a protector who is able to provide a buffer against the malevolence of others and the uncertainty of life. This kind of relationship is also likely to function as an emotional regulator, to help reduce anxiety about his own personal safety. Thus, the primary goods associated with Mr. B's offending appear to be relatedness (i.e., intimacy seeking), mastery (i.e., "educating" boys), possibly creativity (i.e., molding the direction and attitudes of the boys he abuses), pleasure (i.e., sex), possibly affect regulation, and autonomy (i.e., asserting his needs over others).

This formulation points to a number of treatment goals. It is necessary to provide Mr. B with alternative means of securing the goods associated with his offending. This is likely to involve providing him with the capabilities and opportunities to establish consenting intimate relationships with adults, to teach or provide a service to others (adults of course), to acquire alternative outlets for his creativity, and to find other sexual outlets.

Intervention

Based on assessment and matching of static and dynamic risk factors, Mr. B would require intensive treatment and supervision. He would benefit from a high intensity sexual offender treatment program (approximately 12 to 24 months), followed by follow-up maintenance programming. This intensity level reflects Mr. B's moderate to high risk to re-offend (relative to other sexual offenders) and the nature of the dynamic risk factors for which he requires intervention. Similarly, Mr. B's probation/parole supervision needs are intensive, at least initially.

The key in treatment with Mr. B is to invoke change with respect to both his attitudes that support sexual offending and his view of the world. If Mr. B does not begin to regard sexual offending as inappropriate and does not change his worldview, treatment is unlikely to be effective. It is likely that the previous treatment program in which he participated was unsuccessful in preventing re-offending as a consequence of its inability to assist Mr. B to challenge and change his core belief systems, to provide him with a sense of optimism, efficacy, and options to achieve his goals, and to change his life in a positive manner via resolving long-standing vulnerability issues and providing alternatives to securing goods. Once amenability to explore alternatives is created, the dynamic risk factors indicated above are targeted, and strategies later developed when Mr. B has adopted an avoidance goal with respect to sexual offending and positive life goals toward which he is working. Because his offending represents a direct route to obtaining goods, finding alternatives that do not involve abusive behavior should function to alter his behavior.

As noted in Volume I, Mr. B challenges traditional treatment methods, which typically have as a fundamental assumption that individuals must desire to change the targeted behavior in order to benefit from treatment. In addition, traditional treatment methods use techniques such as inducing cognitive dissonance. These techniques will be less effective in engaging Mr. B in the treatment and change processes, since his behavior is congruent with his core belief system. He holds attitudes and beliefs supportive of sexual offending, and actively seeks out offending. He feels no remorse and regards his behavior as acceptable and, in fact, desirable and helpful to others. This does not necessarily indicate psychopathy, but more commonly the belief that his goals are quite legitimate and that their achievement is unlikely to result in harm to himself or others. As such, to engage Mr. B, treatment must appeal to his sense of self-interest (i.e., by appealing to prudential values such as primary goods). As stated in numerous places in this manual, it is necessary for Mr. B to realize that, while the primary goods or values associated with his offending may be acceptable, the means he employs to achieve them are problematic. In a case such as Mr. B, providing treatment using the Good Lives Model as the foundation of treatment has the greatest potential of reaching such individuals and their orientation toward their own self-interest. Using the GLM with Mr. B, we can assist him to work toward achieving goals that do not involve offensive behavior. That is, we assist him to determine that which he seeks to achieve through offending and to identify these needs and find alternative ways of acquiring goods. With respect to treatment process, proceeding in this manner will reduce resistance, as we are not insisting that Mr. B abandon those things which are of value to him, but are rather helping him to meet his needs. In addition to reducing resistance, we are able to increase Mr. B's engagement with treatment, and will subtly begin the process of shifting his attitudes and beliefs should he be amendable to viewing things through the GLM.

Treatment

Generally, individuals following an approach-explicit pathway do not share the treatment provider's goal of ceasing sexual offending. However, given that they do not regard their behavior as wrong, they are likely to freely admit to details of offense behavior. As such, in Mr. B's case, it is not necessary to work with him extensively to obtain information regarding his offenses. However, Mr. B is unlikely to welcome intervention to assist him to change his belief systems, and the treatment provider should expect resistance in this area. A key task is to link his offending related goals to the underlying goods outlined above. This will serve to motivate Mr. B to acquire the skills necessary to live a better, more satisfying life and also to help him develop an understanding of his offending and the purpose it serves.

Using goal setting as an initial task, Mr. B is working toward achieving a desired end (an approach goal) which, as noted previously, is easier to achieve than are avoidance goals. This approach may also be useful as it appears that there are few negative consequences that Mr. B perceives as resulting from his offending. For example, when providing treatment, the negative consequence of imprisonment is often used to increase motivation, and avoidance of returning to prison becomes a treatment goal (via a decisional balance or cost-benefit analysis; Cherry, 2005; Leahy, 2001; Miller & Rollnick, 1991). However, in the case of Mr. B, this is unlikely to be effective, as he is quite comfortable and offends regularly in institutional settings. Essentially, prison offers him ample opportunities to achieve the goods of sex (pleasure), educating and molding others, and some degree of relatedness. Furthermore, he is clearly motivated to offend as a result of the immediate gratification he receives from this. Therefore, he is unlikely to be motivated to refrain from offending by considering longer term consequences which, for him, are not especially salient.

The first steps in treatment are to establish mutually agreed-upon goals, to use the GLM to help Mr. B to envision being in the world in a different way, to determine the primary goods that he seeks to acquire, and to build on his existing strengths to help him achieve these goals. Specifically, although he evidences significant dynamic risk factors for sexual offending, Mr. B does not appear to possess significant life management deficits, such as problems with general self-regulation or impulsivity. Consistent with the approach-explicit pathway, Mr. B demonstrates intact self-regulation. That is, he is able to control his behavior when he so chooses. This is a strength on which treatment can build. Furthermore, Mr. B demonstrates the capacity to form relationships, although (as a result of his core attitudes) he has used this capacity in an inappropriate manner, regarding others as prey rather than as partners. Although he has chosen (as a result of his personal history and consequent attitudes) to use his skills in an offensive manner, the capacity to form relationships can represent a skill on which treatment can build, with the aim of having Mr. B form appropriate, non-offending relationships. In summary, Mr. B possesses skills to achieve primary goods, and also appears to have a strong need to help, protect, and educate others, indicating that these activities hold considerable value for him. One starting point in establishing treatment and good lives goals may be his statement that, while on probation, he had previously contemplated changing his behavior, but did not see any other options for him with respect to a different lifestyle. Treatment could utilize this window of opportunity by building on evidence that (at least once) he had contemplated change. Discovering options and realistic changes may provide the therapist with a starting point while increasing Mr. B's sense of optimism.

During this initial stage of establishing treatment goals, Mr. B also elucidates his larger life goals. *What prompted him to consider, while he was on probation, to "straighten out" his life? What would this life look like? Who would be the important people in this life? What have been some of the obstacles to changing his life? What kinds of activities and experiences does he value most, and why? Into what would he most like to put his energies, and why? Why did he previously think that he was "fooling" himself when he contemplated changing his life?* The objective is to uncover those goods that Mr. B seeks to achieve so that, during treatment, he can develop the capabilities (internal conditions) and opportunities (external conditions) to acquire these goods. For example, Mr. B has stated that he would like to improve his relationship with his mother and would like to develop friendships. Treatment can work toward achieving these goals in addition to targeting criminogenic needs. Mr. B has also stated that he has considered ceasing sexual involvement with boys. It is important that treatment address the issue of that which he would like to obtain with respect to relationships in order that he can eventually acquire a non-offending intimate, or purely sexual, relationship, if this is what he desires. This involves Mr. B appreciating what he seeks and obtains from such relationships, and eventually committing to obtaining these in non-offending ways. As indicated above, this is likely to be quite complex. Given his preference, Mr. B may consider (as a management strategy) becoming involved in relationships with adult men who are youthful in appearance, which may enable him to achieve sexual and intimate gratification with men toward whom he is attracted in consensual relationships. As will be discussed below, this needs to be linked with attitude change, since Mr. B also has a history of preying upon adult males in a coercive manner. In addition, clear behavioral guidelines will need to be established to ensure that he does not re-open opportunities to offend via broadening his relationships to age-inappropriate partners.

The next phase of treatment with Mr. B consists of raising his awareness of the attitudes and beliefs he holds, alongside increasing knowledge of those goods he is attempting to acquire via offending.

In this case, the initial disclosure exercise is used. However, the goals of this exercise are substantively different than with offenders following the other pathways. Specifically, as noted in Volume I, Mr. B is likely to be quite forthcoming in describing his offending behavior in detail because he believes it is acceptable and because his behavior is consistent with his worldview and values. As such, he is unlikely to experience guilt or shame when discussing his behavior and beliefs, and is unlikely to be affected by treatment techniques designed to induce cognitive dissonance, due to this congruence between his attitudes and behavior. With Mr. B, the objective of this disclosure exercise is, therefore, to determine specifically that which he attempts to acquire via offending, the thoughts, beliefs, and emotions associated with his offending behavior, and the frequency and nature of Mr. B's offending and consensual sexual relationships throughout his life. Thus, during this exercise, the therapist will need to interject regularly into Mr. B's narrative, posing questions designed to uncover this information, as he is likely to recount predominantly factual information. *How did Mr. B choose the victims of his offenses? What characteristics, in addition to their vulnerability, appealed to him? How did he arrange access to them? When he met his future victims, did he plan to offend against them, or did this desire develop later? Does his offending behavior differ with boys versus with men? Is there an instance he can recall during which he felt he would like to have a longer term relationship? What is it about his behavior that makes him feel satisfied (other than sexual gratification)?* It is essential that Mr. B respond in a concrete manner, providing details and examples. Also, the therapist should interject in a nonconfrontational manner to ensure that Mr. B does not engage in justifications for his behavior during disclosure.

An additional objective of this exercise is to assess the degree to which deviant sexual arousal and fantasy has played a role in offending behavior and in Mr. B's life, as well as specific information regarding the characteristics of his preferred victim type. *How often does Mr. B engage in deviant sexual fantasy? Does the frequency of deviant fantasy increase prior to offending? Are intimacy and emotional satisfaction ever part of his sexual fantasy? Is there a difference in level of sexual arousal during fantasy to boys versus young men?* This will be a valuable exercise for information gathering and later supervision, given that at this stage in treatment, there is little information available regarding this area.

Following the disclosure exercise, we will have a sense of that which Mr. B values and that which he seeks in life, both generally and via offending. Key questions that should be resolved through this exercise include the impetus for Mr. B's offending behavior. For example, we need to ascertain, independent of his core attitudes and sexual deviance, whether Mr. B's behavior is motivated by a need for intimacy, dominance, a sense of personal power, and so forth. We also need to have a clear understanding of his life goals, in order that we may be able to help him to achieve these goals during treatment. For example, if Mr. B does desire intimacy, treatment will assist him in using his relationship building skills to establish consensual relationships. If Mr. B has a need for dominance or personal power, the therapist needs to assist him to understand the origin of this need and how he can achieve autonomy, safety, and independence without needing to dominate another person. If creativity is an important goal, then exploring alternative outlets is an important therapeutic task. In addition, following the disclosure exercise, both the therapist and Mr. B should have an understanding of his core attitudes toward both life and sexual offending, and the manner in which sexual offending results from these attitudes in conjunction with sexual deviance. In addition, this disclosure exercise will provide the therapist with information regarding those specific situations or circumstances that pose a risk for offending and the warning signs that indicate that re-offending is likely or imminent.

Finally, during the disclosure exercise, Mr. B is required to describe the period of time between his release from prison and commencing offending against his most recent victim (approximately six months), during which he indicated he did not offend, as well as any other non-offending periods of his life. It is essential to understand what was different for Mr. B during these times, as well as effective strategies he may have used to refrain from offending, since these are skills treatment can build upon. In addition, this may reveal times in Mr. B's life during which he was successfully achieving important goals and did not feel the need to offend. If this is the case, part of treatment will involve replicating and expanding these circumstances such that they become the rule rather than the exception. For example, Mr. B may have had a satisfying intimate relationship at this time, may have been able to meet his sexual needs without offending, may have been involved at a meaningful level with important people in his life (such as his mother), or may have been living in an environment that was safe for him and that did not trigger in him the need to dominate and abuse others. The aim is to detect the external conditions associated with appropriate sexual behavior, so that these may ultimately form part of his self-management and good life plans.

Once the therapist and Mr. B have gained an understanding of these factors and his goals, treatment proceeds to inducing attitude change. Typically, at this stage of treatment, the aim is to establish whether sexual offending stems from core attitudes and beliefs that are supportive of sexual offending or arises solely from cognitive distortions that facilitate offending and allow offense progression during the offense process. In the case of Mr. B, it is clear that his core attitudes, including sexual entitlement, hostility, and his belief that the world is a dangerous, "dog-eat-dog" place, lead to offending. Any cognitive distortions evident during the offense process are consequential to these beliefs. As such, the goal of treatment with Mr. B is to change attitudes and core belief systems. Because these attitudes are well-entrenched, and because both Mr. B's beliefs and behavior have been learned and reinforced over an extended period of time, Mr. B must participate in a high intensity treatment program. Mr. B was sexually abused himself by the priests at his school, who were in a position of power and authority. From this experience, Mr. B learned that the world is a dangerous place and that such behavior is a legitimate means by which one gains a sense of control in the world, and consequently adopted this as his way of relating to others. His belief that the world is dangerous is well-founded in his own experience, both during this time and when he was incarcerated. Rather than suffer more abuse, Mr. B took control of his life, as a perpetrator. In addition, his belief that others will suffer in life is grounded in these experiences, leading to both acceptance of his abusive behavior and his view that he is acting as a "protector". As such, it is essential in treatment to recognize that, although abusive, Mr. B's attitudes and worldview have been adaptive for him in that they help him to cope with life as he knows it to be.

In commencing work on attitude change, we start with assisting Mr. B to evaluate the veracity of his views of the world and core beliefs about the world. While the therapist conveys to him the understanding that his views and attitudes have been shaped by his experience, the idea is introduced that other experiences are possible. The aim is to have Mr. B discover and generate instances or examples of times or situations when the world was not a dangerous place, involving both his own personal experiences and those of others. For example, Mr. B could consider times when his mother attempted to protect him from family conflict when he was growing up, as this may represent an instance during which Mr. B could have viewed part of his world as a safer place. Mr. B could be given a "homework" exercise during which he observes the world around him explicitly for evidence that disproves the idea that the world is always a dangerous place. This could be as simple an event as one person helping another who is in need. The aim of such exercises is to allow Mr. B to have experiences during which he views the world differently, and to gain practice being able to see different possibilities other than his usual perceptions of events, which is characterized by hostility and suspicion. Eventually, Mr. B will need to generate alternative interpretations to the events around him, and this type of activity will provide him with needed cognitive and behavioral rehearsal and will slowly begin to erode his hostile belief system.

Part of the attitude change process also involves Mr. B monitoring his interpretation of events around him and situations to which he typically responds with hostility or suspicion. This includes cognitive distortions that arise in situations in which he typically sexually abuses others. He must develop the ability to recognize those situations to which he responds with hostility and to generate alternative interpretations of these events. It is essential that these alternative interpretations are meaningful and realistic for him – that is, interpretations and perceptions that he is be able to believe and view as feasible. This process will be concurrent with the attitude change process described above. Specifically, the process of attitude change is a lengthy and complex one, and Mr. B will need to simultaneously learn to interpret situations differently while challenging his core beliefs about the world. He is likely to experience numerous and frequent setbacks during this process, since his attitudes are long-standing. It is essential that Mr. B receive positive reinforcement for success, by successive approximations, and that the therapist assist him to deconstruct those experiences in which he was unsuccessful. This is done to generate options that would have proved effective and could be implemented in the future.

The above-indicated strategies are designed to alter Mr. B's worldview and core attitudes with respect to the dangerousness of the world and his hostile bias. The attitude change intervention also needs to target beliefs and cognitive distortions specifically associated with his sexual offending behavior. For example, Mr. B believes that the individuals he abuses will eventually be abused by someone, and uses this core belief to justify his offending behavior. He is also unlikely to view himself as having suffered from the abuse he experienced from others. Indeed, at times he is likely to describe it as a positive experience. The aim of attitude change in this area is to have him come to the understanding that sexual abuse is not inevitable, that it does not happen to everyone, as well as to understand that victimization has negative consequences for the victim and does not foster a sense of personal power. This change could be facilitated if Mr. B is able to identify instances during which he experienced a sense of shame or loss of personal power when he was abused. As with Mr. O (see Chapter 7), the aim is not to provide therapy for his own victimization, which should be conducted by a trained and specialized therapist in this area. Instead, the possibility of using his own experiences to assist him to understand the impact of his behavior on the victims of his offenses (and consequently to be able to take an accurate perspective with respect to harm caused to victims) should be explored. This attitude change can also be facilitated by guiding Mr. B to consider the impact of harm caused to victims of sexual offenses outside his target group, such as girl victims or rape, which may be less threatening to him than exploring his own offending at this stage of treatment. Reducing this threat will function to reduce resistance to change. This strategy may also enable him to more easily access victim empathy, as he may not have the same protective cognitive distortions with respect to these types of offenses as he does in relation to the victims of his own offenses. When he is able to view these offenses as inappropriate, the therapist will then move to shifting this view with the aim of generalizing it to the offenses he commits.

Attitude change during treatment also targets Mr. B's sense of entitlement. Obviously, Mr. B gains a sense of personal power through his abuse of others, such as younger inmates when he was in prison, and feels he is entitled to receive services in exchange for protection. Mr. B also selects victims who are vulnerable, including the boys he targeted (the "misfits") and younger, less experienced inmates who may, in fact, be in need of protection. It is possible that Mr. B targets such victims simply because this facilitates the offending process, because he needs to prey on weaker individuals in order to gain a sense of personal power, or because he is attracted to individuals who are vulnerable. As such, the attitude change intervention must be tailored to his motivation for targeting vulnerable individuals, which is unknown at this stage in treatment. Exercises in taking the perspective of others could assist Mr. B in understanding the impact of his behavior derived from his sense of entitlement, which assists in beginning attitude change in this area. From the perspective of the GLM, assisting Mr. B to identify his needs and goals can function to minimize his need to prey on others in order to meet these needs, as well as reduce his need to dominate and to take what he wants from others.

In addition, treatment assists Mr. B to accurately interpret consent in a sexual relationship or encounter. While it can be made reasonably clear that young boys cannot consent to sexual activity due to their age, it would be easy for Mr. B to invoke other cognitive distortions. He may generate other circumstances in which under-age boys could give consent. It would also be easy for him to argue that the younger inmates whom he coerced into sexual activity were able, as adults, to make the decision to consent. Mr. B needs to reach the understanding that other circumstance, such as being young or in a vulnerable situation such as incarceration, can result in the lack of ability to give consent. Mr. B needs to understand that differences in power and vulnerability inhibit the ability to provide consent, and to develop a clear understanding of consent and the ability to recognize when consent is provided and when it is absent.

Concurrent with working on attitude change, during treatment Mr. B also identifies cognitive distortions specifically related to his offending behavior. Once identified, Mr. B develops and rehearses appropriate challenges to these distortions that he will use when he encounters situations that place him at risk or when he begins to think or fantasize about offending. This task will be made easier when the attitude change process has begun and is in progress.

Finally, Mr. B will benefit from learning meta-cognitive techniques (Wells, 2000; Wells & Matthews, 1994, 1996). He is likely to need to use these techniques on a regular basis (initially perhaps daily), in order to be able to monitor his thinking for the presence of offense-supportive patterns and to take immediate preventive action. This entails becoming cognizant of his way of thinking and required changes to this. For example, Mr. B will need to be able to identify when he has returned to thinking about the world in a suspicious or hostile manner, in order that he can implement challenges to this way of thinking immediately, before he begins to think about offending. Such a practice is also implemented with respect to monitoring and challenging thinking that reflects preying on vulnerable others and a sense of entitlement.

As indicated above, the second primary treatment target for Mr. B is deviant sexual arousal/preference. Although confirmatory assessment is recommended, Mr. B clearly demonstrates and expresses deviant sexual arousal to prepubescent and pubescent males. What is not known at this stage of treatment is whether this arousal is preferential, as Mr. B has also offended against adult males. Also, as indicated above, assessment of the content, nature, and frequency of deviant sexual fantasy, is also required. Mr. B will require sexual arousal reconditioning techniques (Marshall et al., 1999; Yates et al., 2000) in order to shift his arousal to age-appropriate partners. This assessment will also include any links to preying on vulnerable individuals as well, although this is unlikely to be a result of deviant sexuality, but rather stems from his core attitudes and personal experience. Finally, Mr. B can be assessed to determine whether he would benefit from medication to reduce sexual arousal (Wettstein, 1998; Yates 2002), although there is no evidence at this stage to suggest that his arousal is excessive or uncontrollable.

Mr. B will need to monitor his sexual arousal, likely for an extended period of time. He will need to avoid situations that place him at risk and avoid access to potential victims. He will also need to ensure that he is able to control deviant sexual arousal, and to re-direct arousal toward appropriate targets. Mr. B must acknowledge that this will continue to pose a risk for him. Likewise, his pre-treatment core attitudes and beliefs, will pose problems in future circumstances. He needs to be prepared to cope with such situations, their associated cognitive distortions and the loss of control. He will also simultaneously continue working toward achieving his goals and acquiring desired goods in a non-offending manner.

Secondary, but important, treatment targets for Mr. B include developing both social and intimate relationships, including supportive social networks and friendships. These can assist him in becoming and remaining offense-free. A Circle of Support network (Wilson & Prinzo, 2001; Wilson et al., 2003) is likely to be particularly helpful in Mr. B's case. Re-establishing his relationship with his mother can also be considered, if this would be supportive and would not interfere with his goals or result in a re-emergence of core hostile and suspicious attitudes. These relationships are developed giving consideration to Mr. B's needs and goals in this area of his life. For example, if Mr. B does not desire to have a long-term intimate partnership, he will need to be assisted to engage in consensual sexual relationships wherein he does not offend.

Maintenance and Supervision

When in a community setting (either during treatment or following treatment while incarcerated), Mr. B would also participate in high intensity supervision (e.g., via parole or probation services) designed to monitor his risk to re-offend and his functioning with respect to maintaining positive attitudinal change. This will also assist in ensuring that his plan for living a better life is running smoothly and that routes to re-offending are not being reopened. Assessment and treatment reports, including risk management plans, are a valuable source for identifying factors that need to be monitored to manage the case. In this case, supervision would entail restricting and monitoring Mr. B's access to prepubescent and pubescent boys, supporting him to establish age-appropriate social and sexual or intimate relationships, and managing deviant sexual arousal and fantasy. As indicated above, Mr. B has not committed any non-sexual offenses. As such, he is unlikely to be at risk to commit offenses of this type, so supervision for this type of behavior is unlikely to be necessary.

Mr. B would benefit from participation in high intensity maintenance programming (i.e., on a weekly basis) after he completes treatment. Supervision should be augmented by regular case conferences between the supervisor and the treatment provider, as this provides multi-source reports on Mr. B's management of his risk factors and his progress toward achieving his good life goals. Facilitating and reinforcing Mr. B's ability to cope with his deviant interest/preference is more likely to be within the domain of the treatment provider, but is also pertinent information for the supervisor. Both the case management and treatment teams can work with Mr. B on the implementation of his good life plan and monitor achievement of good life goals.

As indicated above, the establishment of a Circle of Support (Wilson & Prinzo, 2001; Wilson et al., 2003) may benefit Mr. B in both managing his risk to offending as well as the realization of his good life plan. Members of this group can also provide valuable information on Mr. B's functioning and risk management to parole/probation and treatment providers. This also applies to Mr. B's mother if he has re-established a relationship with her, as well as an intimate partner, if applicable. Mr. B will also need to change his employment such that he does not have access to potential future victims.

Balancing community safety, for example via disclosure, without setting up the offender for failure, requires careful evaluation. Disclosure of offending and risk factors to employers, newly developed networks of acquaintances, and friends must be done cautiously. Mr. B would need to be supported to use his skills to evaluate the potential risks of each circumstance and, when the decision for disclosure is made, manage this in a way that increases the probability of a positive outcome. For example, Mr. B's work supervisor could be apprised of his offenses, in order to assist in monitoring, as well as to assist Mr. B to avoid work social functions at which the children of other employees would be present. As one of his treatment tasks is developing a social network, he will need to be aware that it is likely he will need to disclose his offense history and risk factors to certain people under certain circumstances, and will need to be able to cope with the potential consequences and the threat to goal attainment that this may entail.

Chapter 9: Conclusions

In this volume, we have set out to systematically apply the self-regulation model to the treatment of sexual offenders. In addition, we have attempted to demonstrate the different approaches to treatment that are implemented with offenders following the four pathways proposed by this model. We have integrated treatment within this model with research and best practice that dictates that treatment should be delivered based on comprehensive assessment of risk to re-offend, should target factors that are empirically demonstrated to be associated with sexual offending, and should be relevant to an individual case. We propose that the self-regulation model better enables clinicians to better tailor and implement treatment while taking into account the essential principles of risk, need and responsivity than have previous models of treatment. We also suggest that the integration of these models and practices allows for the use of effective therapeutic approaches and techniques in treatment. We believe the analysis of the four case examples contained in Volume I of this series illustrates both the different treatment approaches required for offenders following different pathways to offending, as well as the application of research-based assessment and practice.

One innovation has been to embed the SRM within the Good Lives Model, a comprehensive, strength based approach to offender rehabilitation. In our view, this model strengthens the SRM and enables therapists to take into account the fact that sex offenders are often pursuing multiple goals when committing offenses. In addition, the multisystemic nature of the GLM means that clinicians are encouraged to formulate cases and implement treatment in a more holistic and integrated manner. The requirement to consider both internal and external conditions means that they do not lose sight of the environmental constraints and facilitators associated with treatment. The consideration of goal acquisition in individual cases allows treatment to adopt a positive orientation that focuses on achieving important life goals, rather than simple avoidance of problematic situations or abandonment of important goals in offenders' lives.

It is anticipated that both of these volumes will provide clinicians with a solid template for assessing and treatment sexual offenders. Of course, additional resources will also be required, including broad assessment models (including risk assessment), specific treatment strategies for dealing with the various criminogenic needs apparent in sex offenders, and the utilization of procedures for modifying deviant sexual preferences where required. However, the structure and suggestions outlined in the two manuals should give therapists an excellent framework for formulating cases and constructing treatments plans to suit particular individuals. In other words, the SRM can function as a comprehensive guide for intervention selection and implementation.

Finally, we would like to briefly address the issue of why the SRM is likely to be such a powerful and effective treatment approach. As described in Volume I, the content and construct validity of the model and its utility in assessing offenders has been the subject of several published papers. It does seem to capture some critical aspects of offenders and their offense processes.

In our view, the SRM works because of its ability to accommodate three very simple but important insights into sexual offending: (a) individuals seek a variety of goals through sexual offending, and utilize various strategies to achieve them; (b) there are different offense trajectories reflecting the fact that these goals are indirectly or directly associated with their offending; and (c) treatment therefore needs to equip offenders with the capabilities to achieve their goals based on these differences in goals and strategies in certain environments. The focus on self-regulation and autonomy concerns gives the model flexibility alongside the ability to accommodate different etiological and treatment models. It is our expectation that future empirical and theoretical work will continue to evaluate and refine the SRM. One message is clear: one size does not fit all. The SRM, by virtue of its inclusion of multiple pathways and goals, is able to deal with the heterogeneity of offenders without losing its shape. It is an integrated, comprehensive, and relatively simple model that is consistent with the fact that human beings are active, meaning seeking, biologically embodied beings who pursue their visions of a good life in a bewildering number of ways. It is also consistent with what we know, at this stage, to be the essential features of effective intervention with these individuals.

References

Ackerman, S. J., & Hilsenroth, M. J. (2003). A review of therapist characteristics and techniques positively impacting on the therapeutic alliance. *Clinical Psychology Review, 23,* 1-33.

Andrews, D. A., & Bonta, J. (1998). *The psychology of criminal conduct.* Cincinnati, OH: Anderson Publishing Co.

Aspinwall, L. G., & Staudinger, U. M. (2003). (Eds.). *A psychology of human strengths: Fundamental questions and future directions for a positive psychology.* Washington, DC: American Psychological Association.

Austin, J. T., & Vancouver, J. B. (1996). Goal constructs in psychology: Structure, process, and content. *Psychological Bulletin, 120,* 338-375.

Beck, A. T., Rush, A. J., Shaw, B. F., & Emery, G. (1979). *Cognitive therapy of depression.* New York: Guilford.

Beck, J. S. (1995). *Cognitive therapy: Basics and beyond.* New York: Guilford.

Beech, A. R., & Fisher, D. (2002). The rehabilitation of child sex offenders. *Australian Psychologist, 37,* 206-214.

Beech, A. R., & Mann, R. (2002). Recent developments in the assessment and treatment of sexual offenders. In J. McGuire (Ed.), *Offender rehabilitation and treatment: Effective programmes and policies to reduce re-offending* (pp. 259-288). Chichester, UK: Wiley.

Bickley, J. A., & Beech, R. (2002). An empirical investigation of the Ward & Hudson self-regulation model of the sexual offense process with child abusers. *Journal of Interpersonal Violence, 17,* 371-393.

Bickley, J. A., & Beech, R. (2003). Implications for treatment of sexual offenders of the Ward and Hudson model of relapse. *Sexual Abuse: A Journal of Research and Treatment, 15(2),* 121-134.

Cherry, S. (2005). *Transforming behavior: Pro-social modeling in practice.* Portland, OR: Willan.

Cumming, G. F., & McGrath, R. J. (2000). External Supervision. In D.R. Laws, S.M. Hudson, & T. Ward (Eds.), *Remaking Relapse Prevention with Sex Offenders: A Sourcebook.* Thousand Oaks, CA: Sage.

Cummins, R. A. (1996). The domains of life satisfaction: An attempt to order chaos. *Social Indicators Research, 38,* 303-328.

Deci, E. L., & Ryan, R. M. (2000). The "what" and "why" of goal pursuits: Human needs and the self-determination of behavior. *Psychological Inquiry, 11,* 227-268.

Deffenbacher, J. L. (1996). Cognitive-behavioral approaches to anger reduction. In K. S. Dobson & K. D. Craig (Eds.), *Advances in cognitive-behavioral therapy.* Thousand Oaks, CA: Sage.

DiClemente, C. C. (1991). Motivational interviewing and stages of change. In W. R. Miller & S. Rollnick (Eds.), *Motivational interviewing: Preparing people to change addictive behavior* (pp. 191-202). New York: Guilford.

Emmons, R. A. (1999). *The psychology of ultimate concerns.* New York: Guilford.

Fernandez, Y. M., Marshall, W. L., Serran, G., Anderson, D., & Marshall, L. (2002). *Group process in sexual offender treatment.* Ottawa, ON: Correctional Service of Canada.

Fernandez, Y. M., Shingler, J., & Marshall, W. L. (2006). Putting "behavior" back into the cognitive-behavioral treatment of sexual offenders. In W. L. Marshall, Y. M. Fernandez, L. E. Marshall, & G. A. Serran (Eds.), *Sexual Offender Treatment: Controversial Issues* (pp. 211-224). New Jersey, NY: John Wiley & Sons.

Friman, P. C., & Finney, J. W. (2003). Time-out (and time-in). In W. O'Donohue, J. E. Fisher, & S. C. Hayes (Eds.), *Cognitive behavior therapy: Applying empirically supported techniques in your practice* (pp. 429-435). Hoboken, NJ: Wiley.

Hanson, R. K. (1996). Evaluating the contribution of relapse prevention theory to the treatment of sexual offenders. *Sexual Abuse: A Journal of Research and Treatment, 8,* 201-208.

Hanson, R. K., & Bussière, M. T. (1998). Predicting relapse: A meta-analysis of sexual offender recidivism studies. *Journal of Consulting and Clinical Psychology, 66,* 348-362.

Hanson, R. K., & Harris, A. J. R. (2004). *The Dynamic Supervision Project.* Ottawa, ON: Public Service and Emergency Preparedness Canada.

Hanson, R. K., Gordon, A., Harris, A. J. R., Marques, J. K., Murphy, W., Quinsey, V. L., & Seto, M. C. (2002). First report of the collaborative outcome data project on the effectiveness of psychological treatment for sex offenders. *Sexual Abuse: A Journal of Research and Treatment, 14,* 169-194.

Hanson, R. K., & Morton-Bourgon. (2004). *Predictors of sexual recidivism: An updated meta-analysis.* (Research Report No. 2004-02). Ottawa, Canada: Public Safety and Emergency Preparedness Canada.

Hanson, R. K., Thornton, D. (1999). *Static 99: Improving Actuarial Risk Assessment for Sex Offenders.* Ottawa: Department of the Solicitor General of Canada.

Heidt, J. M., & Marx, B. P. (2003). Self-monitoring as a treatment vehicle. In W. O'Donohue, J.E. Fisher, & S.C. Hayes (Eds.), *Cognitive behavior therapy: Applying empirically supported techniques in your practice* (pp. 361-367). Hoboken, NJ: Wiley.

Hollin, C. R. (1999). Treatment programs for offenders: Meta-analysis, "what works" and beyond. *International Journal of Law and Psychiatry, 22,* 361-372.

Hudson, S. M., Ward, T., & McCormack, (1999). Offense pathways in sexual offenders. *Journal of Interpersonal Violence, 14,* 779-798.

Kekes, J. (1989). *Moral tradition and individuality.* Princeton, New Jersey: Princeton University Press.

Laws, D. R. (Ed.). (1989). *Relapse prevention with sex offenders.* New York: Guilford.

Laws, D. R. (2003). The rise and fall of relapse prevention. *Australian Psychologist, 38(1),* 22-30.

Laws, D. R., Hudson, S. M., & Ward, T. (2000). The original model of Relapse Prevention with sex offenders: Promises unfulfilled. In D. R. Laws, S. M. Hudson & T. Ward (Eds.), *Remaking Relapse Prevention with sex offenders: A sourcebook* (pp. 3-24). Newbury Park: CA: Sage.

Laws, D. R., & Ward, T. (2006). When one size doesn't fit all: The reformulation of relapse prevention. In W.L. Marshall, Y.M. Fernandez, L.E. Marshall, & G.A. Serran (Eds.), *Sexual Offender Treatment: Controversial Issues* (pp. 241-254). New Jersey, NY: John Wiley & Sons.

Leahy, R. L. (2001). *Overcoming resistance in cognitive therapy.* New York: Guilford.

Levensky, E. R. (2003). Motivational interviewing. In W. O'Donohue, J.E. Fisher, & S.C. Hayes (Eds.), *Cognitive behavior therapy: Applying empirically supported techniques in your practice* (pp. 252-260). Hoboken, NJ: Wiley.

Linley, P. A., & Joseph, S. (2004). Applied positive psychology: A new perspective for professional practice. In P. A. Linley & S. Joseph (Eds.). *Positive psychology in practice* (pp 3-12). New Jersey, NY: John Wiley & Sons.

Mann, R. E., (1998, October). *Relapse prevention? Is that the bit where they told me all of the things that I couldn't do anymore?* Paper presented at the 17th annual Research and Treatment Conference of the Association for the Treatment of Sexual Abusers, Vancouver, BC.

Mann, R. E., & Shingler, J. (2006). Collaboration in clinical work with sexual offenders: Treatment and risk assessment. In W. L. Marshall, Y. M. Fernandez, L. E. Marshall & G. A. Serran (Eds.), *Sexual offender treatment: Controversial issues* (pp. 225-239). New York: Wiley.

Mann, R. E., Webster, S. D., Schofield, C., & Marshall, W. L. (2004). Approach versus avoidance goals in relapse prevention with sexual offenders. *Sexual Abuse: A Journal of Research and Treatment, 16,* 65-75.

Marlatt, G. A. (1982). Relapse prevention: A self-control program for the treatment of addictive behaviors. In R. B. Stuart (Ed.), *Adherence, compliance and generalization in behavioral medicine* (pp.329-378). New York: Brunner/Mazel.

Marlatt, G. A., & Gordon, J. R. (1985). *Relapse prevention: Maintenance strategies in the treatment of addictive behaviors.* New York: Guilford.

Marques, J. K., Nelson, C., Alarcon, J-M., & Day, D. M. (2000). Preventing relapse with sexual offenders: What we learned from SOTEP's experimental treatment program. In D.R. Laws, S.M. Hudson & T. Ward (Eds.) *Remaking relapse prevention with sexual offenders: A sourcebook* (pp. 321-340). Thousand Oaks, CA: Sage Publications.

Marques, J. K., Wiederanders, M., Day, D. M., Nelson, C., & van Ommeren, A. (2005). Effects of a relapse prevention program on sexual recidivism: Final results from California's Sex Offender Treatment and Evaluation Project (SOTEP). *Sexual Abuse: A Journal of Research & Treatment,* 17, 79-107.

Marshall, W. L. (1989). Intimacy, loneliness, and sexual offenders. *Behavior Research and Therapy, 27,* 491-503.

Marshall, W. L. (1999). Current status of North American assessment and treatment programs for sexual offenders. *Journal of Interpersonal Violence, 14,* 221-239.

Marshall, W. L. (2004). Adult sexual offenders against women. In C. R. Hollin (Ed.), *The essential handbook of offender assessment and treatment* (pp. 147-162). Chichester, UK: Wiley.

Marshall, W.L., & Anderson, D. (1996). An evaluation of the benefits of relapse prevention programs with sexual offenders. *Sexual Abuse: A Journal of Research and Treatment, 8,* 209-229.

Marshall, W. L., Anderson, D., & Fernandez, Y. M. (1999). *Cognitive behavioral treatment of sexual offenders.* Chichester, UK: Wiley.

Marshall, W. L., Fernandez, Y. M., Serran, G. A., Mulloy, R., Thornton, D., Mann, R. E., & Anderson, D. (2003). Process variables in the treatment of sexual offenders. *Aggression and Violent Behavior: A Review Journal, 8,* 205-234.

Marshall, W. L., Mulloy, R., & Serran, G. (1998). *The identification of treatment facilitative behaviors enacted by sexual offender therapists.* Kingston, ON: Queen's University, Unpublished manuscript.

Maruna, S. (2001). *Making good: How ex-convicts reform and rebuild their lives.* Washington, DC: American Psychological Association.

McGuire, J. (2002). Criminal sanctions versus psychologically-based interventions with offenders: A comparative empirical analysis. *Psychology, Crime, and Law, 8,* 183-208.

Miller, W. R., & Rollnick, S. (1991). *Motivational interviewing: Preparing people for change.* New York: Guilford.

Miller, W. R., Zweben, A., & DiClemente, C. C. (1992). *Motivational enhancement therapy manual: A clinical research guide for therapists treating individuals with alcohol abuse and dependence* (Project MATCH Monograph Series,Vol. 2). Rockville, MD: National Institute on Alcohol Abuse and Alcoholism.

Murphy, M. C. (2001). *Natural law and practical rationality.* New York, NY: Cambridge University Press.

Newman, C. F. (2003). Cognitive Restructuring: Identifying and modifying maladaptive schemas. In W. O'Donohue, J. E. Fisher, & S. C. Hayes (Eds.), *Cognitive behavior therapy: Applying empirically supported techniques in your practice* (pp. 89-95). Hoboken, NJ: Wiley.

Nicholaichuk, T.P. (1996). Sex offender treatment priority: An illustration of the risk/need principle. *Forum on Corrections Research, 8,* 30-32.

Nicholaichuk, T. P., Gordon, A., Gu,, D., Wong, S. (2000). Outcome of an institutional sexual offender treatment program: A comparison between treated and matched untreated offenders. *Sexual Abuse: A Journal of Research and Treatment, 12(2),* 139-153.

Nicholaichuk, T. P., & Yates, P. M. (2002). Outcome of the Clearwater sex offender program. In B.K. Schwartz & H.R. Cellin (Eds.), *The Sex Offender (Volume IV),* (pp. 7: 1 -18.) Kingston, NJ: Civic Research Institute.

Nussbaum, M. C. (2000). *Women and human development: The capabilities approach.* New York, USA: Cambridge University Press.

Pithers, W. D. (1990). Relapse prevention with sexual aggressors: A method for maintaining therapeutic gain and enhancing external supervision. In W. L. Marshall, D. R. Laws, & H. E. Barbaree (Eds.), *Handbook of sexual assault: Issues, theories, and treatment of the offender* (pp. 343-361). New York: Plenum.

Pithers, W. D., Marques, J. K., Gibat, C. C., & Marlatt, G. A. (1983). Relapse prevention with sexual aggressives: A self-control model of treatment and maintenance of change. In J.G. Greer & I.R. Stuart (Eds.), *The sexual aggressor: Current perspectives of Treatment* (pp.214-239). New York, NY: Van Nostrand Reinhold.

Prentky, R. A. (1995). A rationale for the treatment of sex offenders, Pro Bono Publico. In J. McGuire (Ed.), *What Works: Reducing Re offending – Guidelines from Research and Practice.* New York, Wiley, pp. 155-172.

Prentky, R. A., & Burgess, A. W. (1990). Rehabilitation of child molesters: A cost-benefit analysis. *American Journal of Orthopsychiatry, 60,* 108-117.

Prochaska, J. O., & DiClemente, C. C. (1982). Transtheoretical therapy: Toward a more integrative model of change. *Psychotherapy: Theory, Research, and Practice, 19,* 276-288.

Prochaska, J. O., & DiClemente, C.C. (1986). Toward a comprehensive model of change. In W.R. Miller & N. Heather (Eds.), *Treating addictive behaviors: Processes of change* (pp. 27). New York: Plenum.

Purvis, M., & Ward, T. (2005). *Good lives plans and sexual offending: A preliminary study.* Manuscript in preparation.

Salter, A.C. (1988). *Treating child sex offenders and victims: A practical guide.* California: Sage.

Segrin, C. (2003). Social skills training. In W. O'Donohue, J.E. Fisher, & S.C. Hayes (Eds.), *Cognitive behavior therapy: Applying empirically supported techniques in your practice* (pp. 384-390). Hoboken, NJ: Wiley.

Smallbone, S. W., & Dadds, M. R. (1998). Childhood attachment and adult attachment in incarcerated adult male sex offenders. *Journal of Interpersonal Violence, 13,* 555-573.

Ward, T., & Beech, T. (2006). An integrated theory of sexual offending. *Aggression and Violent Behavior, 11,* 44-63.

Ward, T., Bickley, J., Webster, S. D., Fisher, D., Beech, A., & Eldridge, H. (2004). *The Self-regulation Model of the Offense and Relapse Process: A Manual: Volume I: Assessment.* Victoria, BC: Pacific Psychological Assessment Corporation.

Ward, T., & Gannon, T. (2006). Rehabilitation, etiology, and self-regulation: The Good Lives Model of sexual offender treatment. *Aggression and Violent Behavior, 11,* 77-94.

Ward, T., & Hudson, S. M. (1998). The construction and development of theory in the sexual offending area: A metatheoretical framework. *Sexual Abuse: A Journal of Research and Treatment, 10,* 47-63.

Ward, T., & Hudson, S.M. (2000). A self-regulation model of relapse prevention. In D.R. Laws, S.M. Hudson, & T. Ward (Eds.), *Remaking relapse prevention with sex offenders: A sourcebook* (pp. 79-101). Thousand Oaks, CA: Sage.

Ward, T., Hudson, S. M., & Keenan, T. (1998). A self-regulation model of the sexual offense process. *Sexual Abuse: A Journal of Research and Treatment, 10,* 141-157.

Ward, T., Louden, K., Hudson, S. M., & Marshall, W. L. (1995). A descriptive model of the offense process. *Journal of Interpersonal Violence, 10,* 453-473.

Ward, T., Mann, R., & Gannon, T. (in press). The Good Lives Model of Offender Rehabilitation: Clinical Implications. *Aggression and Violent Behavior.*

Ward, T., & Marshall, W, L. (2004). Good lives, etiology and the rehabilitation of sex offenders: A bridging theory. *Journal of Sexual Aggression, 10,* 153-169.

Ward, T., & Stewart, C. A. (2003). The treatment of sex offenders: Risk management and good lives. *Professional Psychology: Research and Practice, 34,* 353-360.

Ward, T., Vess, J., Gannon, T., & Collie, R. (in press). Risk Management or Goods Promotion?: The Relationship between Approach and Avoidance Goal in the Treatment of Sex Offenders. *Aggression and Violent Behavior.*

Webster, S. D. (2005). Pathways to sexual offense recidivism following treatment: An examination of the Ward and Hudson self-regulation model of relapse. *Journal of Interpersonal Violence, 20,* 1175-1196.

Wells, A. (2000). *Emotional disorders and metacognition: Innovative cognitive therapy.* Chichester, UK: Wiley.

Wells, A., & Matthews, G. (1994). *Attention and emotion: A clinical perspective.* Hove, UK: Erlbaum.

Wells, A., & Matthews, G. (1996). Modelling cognition in emotional disorders: The S-REF model. *Behavior Research and Therapy, 34,* 881-888.

Wettstein, R. M. (1998). *Treatment of offenders with mental disorders.* New York: Guilford.

Wilson, R. J., & Prinzo, M. (2001). Circles of support: A restorative justice initiative. *Journal of Psychology and Human Sexuality, 13,* 59-77.

Wilson, R. J., Prinzo, M., & Picheca, J. E. (2003, October). *Gaining momentum: Professionally-facilitated volunteerism with high-risk sex offenders goes international.* Paper presented at the 22nd Annual Conference of the Association for the Treatment of Sexual Abusers, St. Louis, MO.

Wilson, R. J., Stewart, L., Stirpe, T., Barrett, M., & Cripps, J. E. (2000). Community-based sexual offender management: Combining parole supervision and treatment to reduce recidivism. *Canadian Journal of Criminology, 42,* 177-188.

Wolpe, J. (1990). The practice of behavior therapy (4th Ed.). Elmsford, NY: Pergamon.

Yates, P. M. (2002). What works: Effective intervention with sex offenders. In H.E. Allen (Ed.), *What Works: Risk Reduction: Interventions for Special Needs Offenders.* Lanham, MD: American Correctional Association.

Yates, P. M. (2003). Treatment of adult sexual offenders: A therapeutic cognitive-behavioral model of intervention. *Journal of Child Sexual Abuse, 12,* 195-232.

Yates, P. M. (2005). Pathways to the Treatment of Sexual Offenders: Rethinking Intervention. *Forum, Summer.* Beaverton OR: Association for the Treatment of Sexual Abusers, 1-9.

Yates, P. M., Goguen, B. C., Nicholaichuk, T. P., Williams, S. M., Long, C. A., Jeglic, E., & Martin, G. (2000). *National Sex Offender Programs (Moderate, Low, and Maintenance Intensity Levels)*. Ottawa: Correctional Service of Canada.

Yates, P. M., & Kingston, D. (2005). Pathways to Sexual offending. In B.K. Schwartz & H.R. Cellini (Eds.), *The Sex Offender (Volume V)*, Kingston, NJ: Civic Research Institute, 3: 1-15.

Yates, P. M., & Kingston, D (in press, 2006). Pathways to Sexual Offending: Relationship to Static and Dynamic Risk Among Treated Sexual Offenders. Submitted to *Sexual Abuse: A Journal of Research and Treatment*.

Yates, P. M., Kingston, D., & Hall, K (2003). *Pathways to Sexual Offending: Validity of Hudson and Ward's (1998) Self-Regulation Model and Relationship to Static and Dynamic Risk Among Treated High Risk Sexual Offenders*. Presented at the 22nd Annual Research and Treatment Conference of the Association for the Treatment of Sexual Abusers (ATSA). St. Louis, Missouri: October 2003.

Author Biographies

Tony Ward

Tony Ward Ph.D, M.A. (Hons), DipClinPsyc, is a clinical psychologist by training and has been working in the clinical and forensic field since 1987. He was formerly Director of the Kia Marama Sexual Offenders' Unit at Rolleston Prison in New Zealand, and has taught both clinical and forensic psychology at Victoria, Canterbury, and Melbourne Universities. He is currently the Director of Clinical Training at Victoria University of Wellington. Professor Ward's research interests fall into five main areas: rehabilitation models and issues; cognition and sex offenders; the problem behavior process in offenders; the implications of naturalism for theory construction and clinical practice; assessment and case formulation in clinical psychology. He has published over 170 journal articles, books, and book chapters. His most recent book (co-authored with Devon Polaschek & Tony Beech) is (2006) *Theories of sexual offending,* John Wiley & Sons Ltd.

Pamela M. Yates

Pamela M. Yates, Ph.D., R.D. Psych, is a psychologist by training and has been working as a clinician and researcher since 1987. She has worked with adults and adolescents, including offenders and victims, in numerous jurisdictions across Canada. She has worked at the Correctional Service of Canada since 1996 as a psychologist, clinical director of a high risk sexual offender treatment unit, national manager of sexual offender programs, administrator, and program developer for sexual and violent offenders. Dr Yates research interests include assessment of sexual offense risk and recidivism, treatment development and evaluation, and treatment effectiveness. She has written and co-authored numerous reports and programs in the areas of sexual offending, substance abuse, sex offender assessment and treatment, phallometric assessment, substance abuse, psychopathy, treatment effectiveness, program accreditation, sexual sadism, and the self-regulation model of offending.

Carmen A. Long

Carmen Long, Ed.D., R.D. Psych, is a psychologist who has worked with adult offenders since 1990, and most recently as the national manager of substance abuse programs for the Correctional Service of Canada. Dr. Long's areas of interest are the assessment and treatment of substance abuse and sexual violence, and treatment efficacy. She has co-authored and consulted on prevention programs for substance abuse, sexual offending and general criminality.

ISBN 141209219-1

9 781412 092197